LIST OF CONTENTS.

INTRODUCTION .... G. Oke 3

SOILS AND COMPOST .... J.V.Porter 5 - 7

PROPAGATION .... G. E. Bartlett 8 - 14

GROWING FUCHSIAS .... C. Gubler 15 - 23

BASKETS & HANGING POTS .... D. Boor 24 - 26

STANDARDS .... A. Phillips 27 - 29

TRAINED SHAPES .... G. Oke 30 - 36

MULTI PLANT CULTIVATION .... A. Phillips 37 - 39

GROWING TRYPHLLAS .... P. Heavens 40 - 44

THE FUCHSIA SPECIES .... J. Lamb 45 - 51

ENCLIANDRA FUCHSIAS .... T. Strickland 52 - 53

BONSAI FUCHSIAS .... R. G. Payne 54 - 61

FUCHSIAS IN THE GARDEN .... D. Luther 62 - 66

OVERWINTERING .... P. Boor 67 - 69

GROWING WITHOUT A GREENHOUSE.... B. Price Trasler 70 - 73

HYBRIDISING FUCHSIAS .... G. Rolt 74 - 76

WATERING AND FEEDING .... J. Porter 77 - 78

PEST AND DISEASES .... J. Porter 79 - 85

GLOSSARY .... C. Gubler 86 - 88

APPENDICES

B.F.S. SPECIES LIST .... 89 - 90
B.F.S. HARDY LIST .... 91 - 92
NOTES .... 93 - 94
B.F.S. SALE ITEMS 95

The front cover photograph is Cloverdale Jewel courtesy of Arthur Philips.
The back cover photograph is Border Reiver courtesy of Arthur Phillips.

KT-215-467

First published in Great Britain 2000 by
The British Fuchsia Society
P.O. Box 1068
Kidderminster
DY11 7GZ

ISBN 0 901774 26 X

© The British Fuchsia Society 2000

All rights reserved. No part of this publication may
be reproduced, stored in a retrieval system, or
transmitted in any form or by any means, electronic,
mechanical, photocopying, recording or otherwise,
without the prior permission of the
publishers, The British Fuchsia Society.

Printed in Great Britain by
Bookcraft (Bath), Ltd, Midsomer Norton

ALL ABOUT FUCHSIAS.

This book was first published in 1993 by the British Fuchsia Society, to provide information for you on the growing of Fuchsias. This second addition printed in 2000 has been rewritten to include many of the old tried and tested methods along with many new innovative methods.

Whether you have been growing fuchsias for some years or are just a beginner there are plenty of topics covered to help you improve your cultural techniques or to open up many new avenues for you to try.

This book has been written by members of the British Fuchsia Society who have been growing fuchsias for many years and have a wealth of knowledge, experience and advice to offer. As a source of reference covering all aspects of growing fuchsias from hybridising, selecting your plants, training to your desired shape, species, compost, pest and diseases you will find this book invaluable.

I would like to thank George Bartlett, Carol Gubler, John Porter, Di. Boor, Peter Boor, Arthur Phillips, Paul Heavens, Derek Luther, Barbara Price Trasler, Jack Lamb, Trevor Strickland, Gwen Rolt, Roy Payne and Arthur Tickner for their contributions.

The front cover photograph of Cloverdale Jewel was hybridised by Cliff Gadsby in 1974.
The back cover photograph of Border Reiver was hybridised by Dr. Matthew Ryle in 1980.

For further information about the British Fuchsia Society please contact the Secretary.

G. Oke.

President
Mr. J. Muil

Secretary:
The British Fuchsia Society,
PO Box 1068,
Kidderminster,
DY11 7GZ.

Editor:
G. Oke,
2, Lichfield Avenue,
Evesham,
Worcs.
WR11 5EA

© 2000

SOILS AND COMPOSTS.

By J.V.Porter.

It has often been thought and said by amateur growers that "the top showmen/women must have a secret formula they use for their potting compost" thinking that this "secret" enables them to grow the best plants. This in general, is just not the case, however it is true to say, that the better growers use a potting compost that suits their method of growing.

What is compost? For the raw beginner it can be most confusing when they read or hear about the various formulae and mixes used in the hobby of growing fuchsias. Firstly, the correct term we should use is "potting compost" this defines it from the word "compost" which is a heap of rotten vegetative matter at the bottom of the garden. Potting compost is a mixture made up of ingredients suitable for growing plants in pots. Very often a fuchsia grower will say "compost" when they mean "Potting compost" myself included.

At one time the mixtures were made up by the gardeners themselves using loam, leaf mould, peat, manure, grit, bone meal etc., however in 1933 science took a hand in formulating potting composts, this was at the John Innes Research Station who, after much testing, produced potting compost formulae for seed sowing, and potting mixtures numbered 1, 2 and 3. which are made up with; 7 parts sterilised loam, 3 parts peat, 2 parts grit and fertilisers added at different rates for the different mixes. I can well remember a bucket of loam on the gas cooker steaming away for a few hours, the smell was atrocious. This action killed all the loam borne pests and fungi. John Innes composts served the gardeners well for many years in fact some growers still try and use a similar formula, the only difficulty being the quality of the loam.

Eventually the problem of obtaining a good quality loam and the somewhat messy business of sterilising it, even commercially, resulted in a need for a replacement or substitute potting compost being found. Science began to look for other ways of growing plants in pots, Research at the University of California in the late 1950's produced a formula based on peat alone, this was the start of what we now call soiless potting composts. It is true to say that pot and container plants nowadays, travel much greater distances from their origins than ever before, by road and air transport, so consideration of weight is also a prime factor in any new potting compost.

Since the 50's other soiless potting composts have been made from materials such as bark, fibreglass, rock wool, sawdust, household waste, coir etc., etc. I would say that at the present time at least 90% of amateur fuchsia growers use a soiless potting compost based on peat.

Peat like loam varies in quality depending on it's source of excavation, for instance; peat from Finland is light and fluffy and said to be a young peat (only 2 or 3 million years) peat from Somerset tends to be black and is called sedge peat, on it's own it is not very good for use in pots, because of it's poor drainage qualities, peat from Ireland is called sphagnum moss peat and in my opinion is the best. However, manufacturers of potting composts nowadays often mix a *blend* of the various peats available to them.

A key factor in producing a potting compost is to ensure that the acidity or alkalinity is at the correct level for the plants it is being produced for, this is known as the pH level. It is said that fuchsias prefer a pH level of 7, which is actually neutral, with below 7 being acid and above 7 being alkaline. Raw peat when excavated usually has a pH level of between 2.5 and 4.5 the compost producers add enough lime in order to lift the pH value to between 5.5 and 6.5. This level of acidity has proved excellent for fuchsias. With the addition of the manufacturers own formula of fertilisers, which is usually quite high in nitrogen to make plants grow, the potting compost is ready for the gardener's use.

Although manufactured potting compost is perfectly alright to use just as it is, straight from the bag, as indeed most commercial nurseries do use it that way, amateur fuchsia growers have a tradition of adding other ingredients to *improve* it's performance. Drainage is the excuse for this adding tradition. Inert materials such as washed grit, perlite, vermiculite, polystyrene beads etc., are the usual favourites and will be added to the potting compost at a ratio of 5 parts compost to 1 part drainage additive. It must be remembered that adding drainage to the potting compost is in itself a good idea, but the better the drainage the quicker the potting compost will dry out, especially on warm days, therefore, if the plants are left unattended all day, some form of automatic watering will be needed.

Some fuchsia growers like to mix their own potting compost by purchasing all the ingredients separately, this enables them to mix just the right amount needed for use at any given time. Ensuring that the potting compost is always fresh and has not been standing in a garden centre for several months. Base fertilisers, lime and peat can be bought from any good garden centre or store, complete with the fertiliser manufacturers instructions for making potting compost. Chempak and Vitax are two of the companies who offer these products. One of the slight problems with this *mix your own* system comes when the potting compost has become too dry. Purpose made potting composts have a wetting agent mixed into the potting compost which enables water to permeate through the potting compost when watered. The mix your own system, will not have a wetting agent mixed in and watering can become difficult. However this can be overcome, by either adding a little washing up liquid to the water or standing the dry plant in a bucket of water for a few minutes, until the potting compost has become moist enough, *a word of warning here,* do not over-wet any fuchsia that has dried out almost to a wilt. Placing the plant in a shady spot of the garden and water a little at a time, spreading the watering over a few hours is the safest way to avoid root problems or in some cases the death of the plant.

In recent years pressure has been brought on the garden industry to limit the use of peat, this has resulted in a number of peat substitutes being tested and marketed. The most common of these are coir (coconut fibre) tree bark in different grades, sawdust, household waste, rock which has been heat treated to produce materials such as vermiculite, perlite and rockwool. etc,. These potting composts are made up with either one single compound or a mixture of more than one, plus fertiliser. It is certainly possible to grow successfully with these potting composts but they are different from peat or loam, and just as the growers of the 50's and 60's had to gain experience with the use of soiless potting composts, modern growers also need experience and practice with these modern potting composts, before they can be generally accepted as a substitute.

SEED SOWING and ROOTING CUTTINGS.

For seed sowing and rooting cuttings, manufacturers usually add sharp sand, vermiculite or perlite to a finer grade of peat and a less amount of fertiliser. However it is possible to use any ordinary potting compost without any problems, other than perhaps one or two larger lumps of peat being in the way of the seed or cutting being inserted, these can easily be removed by hand.

It must be remembered that with plants in pots and containers the fertiliser content of any potting compost will eventually deteriorate either by leeching away with watering or even used up by the plants. Once this has happened, and it can be as little as five weeks from being potted, supplementary feeding is absolutely necessary with fuchsias. The subject of feeding is covered in another chapter.

PROPAGATION.

By G.E.Bartlett.

If any growers of fuchsias were asked what it was that endeared Fuchsias to them more than any other attribute, I am sure that the answer would come back "The ease with which new plants can be obtained from older plants".

Yes, it is very easy to increase your stock and to provide sufficient spare plants for activities such as Plant Stalls, Plant swops etc. etc. It is possible, with a minimum of effort, expense and expertise, to obtain one hundred per cent success when rooting cuttings. There are no set rules that you have to follow, in fact, as has been said on many occasions by speakers around the country, growing fuchsias is not a scientific art.

It is Nature's intention that any piece detached from a plant shall form roots, if given the right type of conditions, in an effort to ensure that the species shall not be eradicated. We can make use of Nature to increase our stock of plants. But why, when a piece is detached from a plant, do roots start to form. What is the Chemistry behind this process? Not being a Botanist I am unable to give a succinct answer to these questions. I am led to believe that it is all tied up, as usual, with hormones. It is stated that the hormonal activity necessary for the formation of the roots is greatest at the very tips of each shoot and that this concentration of hormones is reduced as it passes down each shoot just beneath the surface of the skin. It therefore follows that if we remove pieces from the very ends of each shoot, the hormonal activity being at its greatest, the possibility of rooting taking place will be at its best.

What, though are the right conditions to encourage rooting. Basically we need two things, warmth and moisture. If we can provide these, then we stand a good chance of success. Notice that the word used is warmth and not heat. I am sure that more failures occur when attempting to root fuchsia cuttings by giving them too much heat than for any other reason. A gentle warmth of about fifteen degrees Celsius (sixty degrees Fahrenheit) will be sufficient. Moisture can be obtained from the tap so provides no difficulty. If we can provide a place for our cuttings where a humid atmosphere can be maintained so that our cuttings do not lose their turgidity, then we should be able to guarantee success. So let us go through the process step by step. We will require suitable cutting material. We will also need some compost, a container for the cuttings, a sharp knife, razor blade or scalpel, labels and a watering can with a fine rose.

CUTTING MATERIAL. As stated earlier the very tips of each shoot stand the best chance of rooting, although longer pieces and leaf axil buds will also succeed. Ensure though that the stock plant from which the cuttings will he removed is itself a good example of the type of plant you require. A good healthy plant will provide good healthy progeny. Ensure that the parent plant has been well watered a couple of hours before removing the cuttings so that every part of the plant is completely charged with moisture.

The size of the cutting will depend on your own subsequent experience, but I would suggest that a small green tip cutting, which consists of one pair of mature leaves, one immature pair and a growing tip, will be excellent for our purpose. If it is possible to find a shoot growing with the leaves growing in sets of three, as opposed to the usual two, then use those for your cuttings. When at a later stage, the plant is being trained, you will obtain three branches from each set of nodes instead of two, an increase of fifty per cent more branches. I prefer to sever the cutting by using a sharp 'hobby' knife and cutting just above a leaf node. Other growers remove the cutting by severing beneath the leaf node and then trimming off the lower leaves. Both methods work equally as well but by severing above the leaf node new shoots can form from the leaf axil left on the plant. One suggestion, do not remove your cuttings from the parent plant until everything has been prepared. At no time do I wish the cuttings to lose their turgidity i.e. to wilt. So let us make sure that everything else is ready.

COMPOST. There is always considerable discussion as to the right type of compost which should be used for the successful striking of cuttings. There are two schools of thought. The first is that, as has already been stated, the basic requirements for success being warmth and moisture, there will be no need for the compost to contain any nutrient. Rooting will take place and a good root system will form quickly as the plant will anxiously search for food.

The second is that the compost can contain a diluted amount of nutrient and that the roots, when formed, will be able to use this nutrient to build up a good plant. For those of us who are not perhaps in a position of being able to individually pot on the rooted cuttings as soon as a satisfactory root system has been formed, I would recommend using a compost containing some nutrient. I use my ordinary potting compost mixed with an equal proportion of Vermiculite. The vermiculite contains no nutrient but it has the advantage of being very soft and also can absorb its own volume of water, a further advantage is that later it will also act as a reservoir for any liquid feed we may add. It is possible to root fuchsias in any type of medium provided that moisture is present, so pure water, moist sand, moist Perlite, moist Vermiculite etc. will all provide the necessary foundation.

PROPAGATORS. There is no need to go in for expensive, thermostatically controlled, propagators. Although if such equipment is available - excellent. It is possible to purchase, relatively cheaply, seed tray sized propagators with electric heating elements built into their bases. These are excellent although I do find they provide a temperature rather higher than the one I desire. Larger, two seed tray sized propagators are available and these generally speaking have a thermostat which you can set at the level you require. Perhaps more convenient for the majority of those without the facilities of a greenhouse, are the windowsill type of heated propagators. These are excellent, they do not clash with the normal house furnishings, and are extremely successful.

Provided we can supply an environment which can maintain a relatively high humidity then we should get success even without the added advantage of electrical heating. Such humidity can be obtained by using enclosed containers such as coffee jars, jam jars, sweet jars, lemonade bottles or even plastic bags. Let your imaginations wander in your search for "do it yourself" equipment.

CONTAINERS. These can be as diverse as the propagators. Yogurt pots (with holes cut in the base), small flower pots, small margarine tubs (again with drainage holes), strips of 'Plantpak' seedling trays, in fact anything which will fit into your propagators.

Now let us get down to the method. Mix up your compost and get it as fluffy as possible by letting it trickle through your fingers (a bit like mixing pastry). Ensure that it is just moist so that when the cuttings are watered in later, the moisture will be immediately taken up. Place some compost in the containers but do not firm it in any way.

Remove the cuttings from the parent plant and gently insert them into the compost. It is often recommended that you should make a hole with the dibber and then gently firm the compost around the base of the cuttings. I do not find that this is necessary as no damage is caused to the base of each cutting if the compost is light and fluffy. I just push the cuttings into the compost. You will probably have noticed that I have not mentioned using Hormone Rooting powders or liquids, this is because I do not personally use them. With cuttings of this type rooting will take place without such assistance. However the harder type of cutting might benefit from using them. If you are in the habit of using these products, by all means carry on doing so., If they give you added confidence then they are doing good.

When you have filled your container with one variety of plant ensure that a label bearing the name of the plant is in position. I also add the date to the label so that a record is kept of when each cutting was struck. Water in the cuttings using the fine rose on a watering can. This will have the effect of settling the compost around the cuttings and will be all the watering necessary for some time. Place your container of cuttings within your chosen propagator. If you have a sealed container such as a coffee jar or a sweet jar, screw on the end and your task is completed.

If your propagator is not of the sealed type then it will be necessary to spray the cuttings at regular intervals to keep them turgid. It is important to prevent any wilting of these cuttings so ensure that they are placed on a window sill or in a greenhouse where they will be out of the direct rays of the sun. Preferably, if growing these cuttings indoors, use a window sill which does not receive the full rays of sunshine. A north facing window, in a cool room, will be very suitable. A sheet of newspaper will provide sufficient protection if needed.

Now it is a question of patience. At a temperature of about fifteen degrees Celsius or (sixty degrees Fahrenheit) the cuttings will take three to four weeks to root. Slightly higher temperatures will speed up the process, but too high a temperature may lead to complete failure. Those cuttings in sealed containers will require no attention whatsoever. Do not take them out to water as they will not require it, the moisture contained within the compost and the sealed unit cannot escape and will be recycled. Similarly, a change of air is not necessary as the plants natural cycle of using oxygen by night and carbon dioxide by day, will provide all that is required. When the cuttings have rooted it will be noticed that the centres take on a fresh green look and are looking decidedly perkier. When this stage has been reached they can be taken from their propagators and potted individually into small pots. An examination of the root system will provide proof of success of your propagation.

Bearing in mind that the only two important commodities are moisture and warmth we can slightly amend the method used by countless growers over the years who have rooted their fuchsias cuttings in a jar of water on the windowsill. The criticism of this method has always been that the root system thus formed is brittle by nature and that difficulty is experienced when transferring the root system into a pot of compost.

Instead of using a jar of water a block of OASIS (wet type) can be used as the medium into which we root the cuttings. Brick sized blocks of oasis can be purchased quite cheaply and will supply us with a number of 'slices' each of about an inch thickness. Remove a slice of oasis and in one flat side score partially through the block so that you have eight almost separate small blocks which can each take one cutting. Soak the oasis so that it is completely saturated with pure water.

Cuttings can now be removed from your parent plant in the usual way and gently inserted into the oasis. With slightly harder stems it may be possible to push them into the wet oasis but it might be preferable to use a cocktail stick or something similar to make a small hole in the oasis and to just slip the cutting into that. Each cutting can have its own label or the block can be filled with cuttings all of the same cultivar.

The block of oasis can now be placed in a container (I find that Ice Cream tubs are excellent for this purpose) a small quantity of water poured into the container and then placed on the windowsill or wherever it is intended you should root these cuttings. There is no need to enclose the container in a plastic bag, unless you prefer to do so, as the water in the container will give the required humidity around the cuttings to keep them turgid. Shade from the hot sun. After three or four weeks roots will probably be seen emerging around the sides of the oasis block. At this stage I usually tip away the water in the container and replace it with a dilute fuchsia liquid food (Chempak No.3. or Chempak Fuchsia Food is ideal).

After a further week it will be possible to separate the cuttings from each other and give them their own individual pots of compost. It is very easy to separate them by just breaking the oasis where you have made the 'score' marks. Any roots which have passed into the neighbouring cutting's oasis will just slip out. Pot each individually making no attempt to remove the root system from the oasis but bury the complete block of oasis plus roots in your pot of compost ensuring that no part of the OASIS is above the surface of the compost. Failure to carry out this simple rule will mean that the moisture will be leached from the oasis and the roots contained within it are likely to be 'pinched'.

Even though the cuttings have virtually rooted in water they will suffer no setbacks whatsover and will continue to grow and produce fine plants for you. I have no idea what happens to the OASIS around the base of the plant, whether it disintigrates or remains intact, but either way the plant continues to thrive.

AUTUMN CUTTINGS - HARD WOOD CUTTINGS.

A further method well worth trying as it can provide you with an early supply of soft wood cuttings in the Spring is to take hard wood or 'stick' cuttings in the Autumn.

In late September or early October before the onset of severe frosts some of the mature branches of your 'hardy' fuchsias can be removed and used as cutting material. Trim each stem so that you have a length of up to 30cm (12") (more if you so desire) and carefully defoliate by cutting away the leaves - I suggest cutting away the leaves so that there is no risk of damaging the dormant buds in the leaf axils. When left with a clear stem it is helpful to slightly wound the base of the 'stick' by tapping it with a sharp knife - just cutting through the surface of the skin. The wounded end can be dipped in a hormonal rooting powder or liquid. Five or six such cuttings can be pushed into a 9cm (3.5") pot of your usual compost (I use a multi purpose compost with an equal amount of Vermiculite). When in position and labelled, the compost can be settled by watering with a fine rose on a watering can and the pot can be placed in the corner of a greenhouse where a frost free temperature can be maintained.

Winter care consists of ensuring that the compost does not dry out and an overhead spraying will help to keep the dormant buds nice and soft. Rooting can take several weeks but it is possible by this method to have cutting material of sufficient size for the first batch of soft green tipped cuttings in January and February.

These little 'mother plants' can later be planted either separately or as a group in larger pots and will provide a good patio display.

I have concentrated on small green tip cuttings. The method of rooting any type of cutting is precisely the same although longer cuttings may take a greater period of time before roots start to form. Experiment with differing cuttings. Practically any piece of fuchsia will root if given the type of containers which have been described. I have also concentrated on fuchsias by the cutting method, which is the only way of ensuring the plant developed from the cutting is identical with the mother plant. There are other methods of increasing stock by grafting, but these are the domain of the more experienced grower. It is also possible to increase the stock of the species by growing them from seed. The seed obtained from the cultivars will not result in identical plants to the mother, and most of the plants raised using this method are inferior.

Types of Cuttings

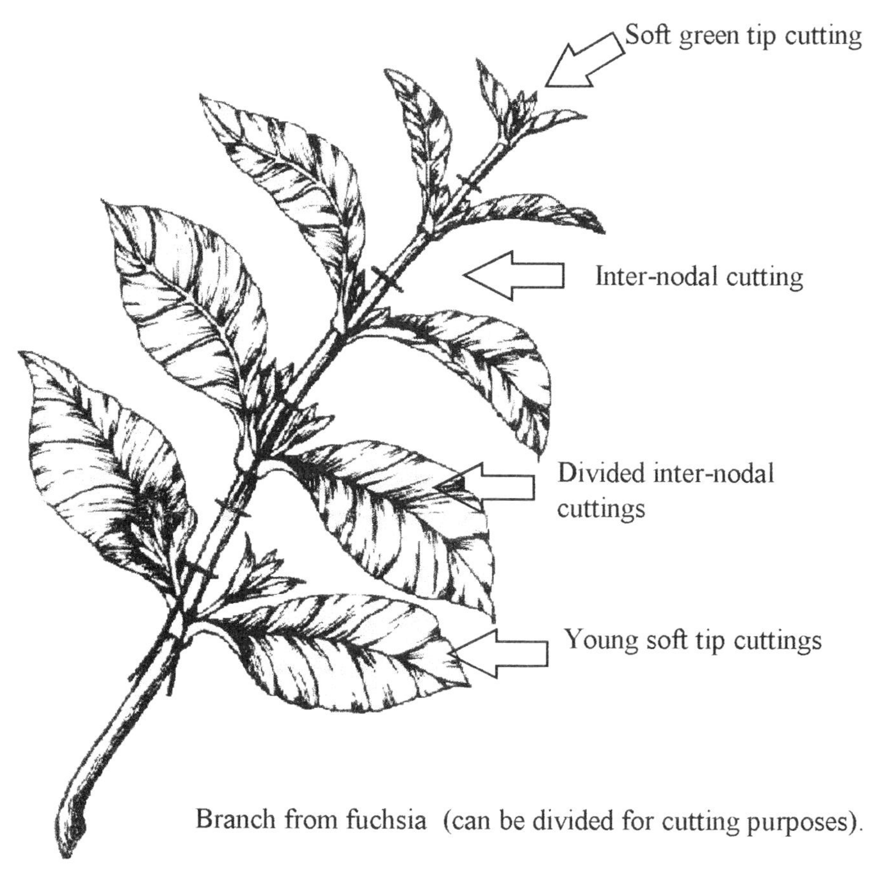

Branch from fuchsia (can be divided for cutting purposes).

GROWING FUCHSIAS

By Carol Gubler

A visit to a fuchsia show or display, a look round a garden, admiring a hanging basket or pot will so often tempt anyone and everyone to enter the world of fuchsias. However, whilst there are rules for showing, there are no such rules for growing fuchsias. Unfortunately, it is not a case of saying do this or do that, such an approach might be feasible if all of our growing and allied conditions were identical, but this is obviously not the case. Our greenhouses or growing facilities can vary so much - greenhouses are of different sizes, construction and position and conditions in these greenhouses vary enormously. Most importantly, the time that is available as well as the dedication and application which can be generated, depends on the enthusiasm of the individual. Thus an article such as this, which is aimed at all growers, can only generalise and offer guidance. The rest is left to the grower to experiment and adapt according to their facilities and resources - if in doubt ask at either a local fuchsia society, specialist nursery or the man down the road that grows those magnificent plants!

It must be stressed that all the growing methods discussed in the rest of this piece are generalisations since, for example, it is quite as feasible to grow excellent plants from a current year cutting as from a plant that is two or three years old.

BUSH STYLE GROWTH.

A bush style growth is ideal for pots and tubs etc. and can be thought of as a plant which may be grown on a short single stem, or a more shrubby growth with a number of shoots produced from below soil level - grown either from one or more plants, both types should have a balanced all round growth. Previous year's plants are regarded as plants from cuttings rooted in the previous year, and except for late cuttings (see below), they have the characteristic of having seasoned woody growth by the end of their first year. Such plants can be split into clearly defined groups.

(a). Cuttings taken early in the year which provide plants for 13 cm and smaller pot sizes, the former being from cuttings taken very early in the year and the latter in early spring. In the autumn they are allowed to become dormant by reducing watering and are placed in a cooler part of the greenhouse. The leaves need to be removed from the woody stems and it is preferable for this action to be done manually, rather than leaving wholly to nature. Removing them manually, means you remove the pests and diseases, such as rust, that often hibernate on the leaves, which can become a nuisance the following year. It must be stressed that although watering is reduced, the plants must not be allowed to dry out completely, and the temperature must not be allowed to fall below freezing point. If the plants have developed long stems, it is beneficial to cut them back by about a half to produce a good woody structure. If your facilities allow and your greenhouse can be kept between 3°C and 5°C (38° and 40°F)then a harder prune can provide spectacular results - if your greenhouse is going to be cooler then a light prune allows for a little winter die back. In the following year, they are reactivated - if they have not already started to grow - by bringing them into the light and spraying with lukewarm water. If they have had a truly dormant season, then when new growth is seen the plants can be hard pruned to just above the active growth to form a compact woody structure, which will provide the foundation for the current year's growth. In the autumn the plants are repotted by teasing away as much of the old soil as possible and potting them down into a smaller pot - some root pruning may be necessary to achieve this. They will take up less room in your greenhouse and during repotting you will be able to cheek the roots for Vine Weevil and remove any grubs that you may find. In the spring the plants are then progressively grown on until they reach their current year's potential, both in pot size and top growth.

(b) Cuttings taken in late spring and early summer, which are grown on to reach 11cm (4½”) or 13cm (5¼”) pots by the end of the growing season are not allowed to flower. They are stopped at every two sets of leaves to build up substantial plants of seasoned growth by the autumn. The normal rules for good cultivation are followed from the cutting stage onwards - the plants are grown in humid conditions, regularly turned to secure all round growth, generally fed with a balanced fertiliser to ensure controlled steady growth and kept clean of pests and diseases. In the autumn, the plants take up their winter quarters on a staging in full light, with a minimum temperature of 5°C (40°F) or thereabouts. The aim is that the plants do not go dormant, but just tick over and whilst defoliation is not necessary (although some growers practice it), it is important however to remove yellowing leaves promptly. At the first hint of longer day length and warmer conditions - hopefully in January - the plants quickly show new signs of growth. In view of their treatment the previous year very little pruning is required, merely a tidying up operation to ensure well shaped plants. Thereafter it is necessary to repot them, whilst avoiding as much damage as possible to the fibrous roots. The plants are then progressively potted on to 15 cm pots or even larger, or can be used for basket work. This manner of growth is known as the biennial system and is both an economical and reliable method of producing fine quality plants.

(c) Cuttings taken after the end of June, will generally be green plants, in small pots with a little or no woody growth, by the end of the summer. This means that during the winter months, they will require the very best of conditions with maximum light and a temperature of approximately 8°C (46°F). Lower temperatures and/or poor light, lead to weak growth and leaf drop. The aim is slowly to grow on the plants, and when conditions improve pot them into a larger pots to produce fine specimen plants. Many a fine plant can be grown from cuttings either grown on like this or purchased early from a nursery - with two or three stops a fine show can be produced.

Plants which have reached a 15cm (6") pot by the end of the growing season are normally only to be considered for possibly one more year in a 15cm (6") pot. Subsequently they require larger pots, and their treatment in winter is the same as described in (a). Keeping plants as they age to a smallish pot will invariably lead to a deterioration in both leaf and flower - so gradual progression to larger pots is recommended.

THE GREENHOUSE - OR EQUIVALENT!

The maintenance of congenial conditions for our plants, which involves the provision of humidity, the control of temperature and the movement of air is necessary at all times. Bringing together the right proportion of these requirements creates the correct atmosphere. In late winter and early spring the aim is to raise the temperature and to provide a very low level of humidity compatible with the plants being grown.

A cold damp environment must be avoided. As the season progresses the emphasis changes, so that by late spring onwards, according to the weather conditions, it is necessary to think about holding the temperature down to around 21°C (70°F) and to increase the humidity content of the air. The hand spray plays an important part in these proceedings at the commencement of the growing year it is used sparingly, mainly to encourage new growth. Its use is increased gradually until by late spring it is used extensively, not only over the plants, but also on the staging and the floor, maybe two or three times per day, if possible. This approach not only provides the higher humidity levels, but also reduces temperature. Allied with the spraying is the careful use of the vents and doors to provide the necessary changes and movement of air - but avoid the creation of draughts. Throughout the growing season, as with the spraying procedure, be guided by the overall weather conditions, so that even during the winter months when the weather is suitable, vents and/or doors can be opened for short periods until in the spring they can be opened fully during daylight hours.

Linked with the foregoing is the light factor, for which the rules are quite simple. During the early growing season there is a need for maximum light for the established plants, so that weak and straggly growth is avoided. By early summer, maximum light will mean that on sunny days, the temperature will rise dramatically. Therefore, at this time the reduction of temperature rather than maximum light becomes of importance and so the green house should he shaded.

Because of our climate we are forced to house our plants under glass until late spring or early summer. Thereafter it is much better to locate established plants out of doors in a sheltered position, where they can receive the sun for part of the day. Generally plants produce healthier growth in such conditions, and they tend to avoid the problems associated with greenhouse growing. Spraying and other disciplines such as turning the plants on a regular basis must still be maintained.

FEEDING & COMPOSTS

The importance of feeding plants throughout the growing season cannot be emphasised too much - feeding allows your plants to be grown to their highest potential - whether they do so rests with you. The number of different feeds as well as composts around can be bewildering and the choice is very much yours. Feed wise - manufacturers are required to provide an analysis of their components on the container, which is known as the NPK ratio (N for nitrogen, P for phosphorous and K for potash). Composts can vary from loam based, peat based or whatever - all I can do is suggest that you find something that suits your style of growing, do not necessarily purchase the cheapest or the bags that look a little old and battered. Every fuchsia grower will tell you something different about composts - perhaps to add grit, others will tell you to add vermiculite or perhaps something different. Ultimately the choice is yours! Find something or a mix that suits you and stick with it, all the compost does is hold the roots in position, the feed makes the difference between a good fuchsia and a great one.

At all times never give more than the recommended strength in a 7 day period and in winter/early spring the period can be 14 or 21 days. The feed regime that is generally recommended is a balanced feed throughout the growing season 20:20:20. In spring to promote growth it may be necessary to give an occasional high nitrogen feed with a ratio of 20:10:10. However on most occasions a balanced feed seems to give the best results promoting not only good growth but continual flowering during the summer months.

In the amount of space available, I have only been able to touch on the subject and deal with generalities.

PLANT TURNING AND POTTING ON

Plants always grow towards the light so the grower has to try and ensure that if plants are to have an even all round growth, it is necessary that all plants, standards and baskets are turned through 90 degrees - every 2 or 3 days. If an imbalance starts to occur and growth is becoming more pronounced on one side than the other, it can be corrected by amending the turning procedure until the problem is rectified.

Turning the plants ensures that the grower becomes acquainted with the plants and will spot any disease or insect problem in the early stages. Examining the plants as they are turned allows for the removal of yellowing or damaged leaves, the correction of unbalanced growth, and whether the plant needs more water or perhaps potting on. Each plant can be treated as an individual, ensuring that they get what they need, rather than being treated as part of the mass. Always have the labels facing in the same direction so that it is easy to spot which plants have been turned.

One of the secrets of success, early in the growing year, is to keep only the very best plants and discard those not coming up to expectations. It may sound rather ruthless, but your time will be much better spent concentrating on fewer good plants rather than a collection of poor to moderate plants. Above all, remember that plants need room and cannot give of their best if they have to exist in cramped conditions. This is something you will hear many keen fuchsia growers say - but in my experience it is easier said than done!

It is customary to pot on in stages i.e. from a 11cm (4¼") pot to a 13cm (5 -5¼"), 13cm (5 - 5¼") to 15cm (6") etc. After that the graduation can be increased. This generally means that a plant which ends its first full season in a 15cm (6") pot will have had four additions of new compost. The gradual addition of compost is believed to be more beneficial than moving straight from a small pot to a large pot, since the plant will not be able to make good use of the excess compost, which will become leached of nutrients and tend to become waterlogged

It is often advisable when potting on to use the "pot in pot" method as this involves less damage to the structure and roots of the plant. Remove the plant gently from the original pot, place a little compost in an appropriately sized larger pot, place the pot that you have just removed from the plant in the larger pot and gently pour compost into the gap between the two, a little pressure on the sides of the inner pot will ensure that a mould of compost is made. Remove the inner pot and place the root ball into the mould. A slight tap will ensure that any gaps are closed then add a little more compost and your plant will not even notice that it has been moved.

Potting on is obviously necessary if the plant has not reached the desired size pot in which you wish it to flower. The signal to pot on is when the roots are running freely through the compost. Any marked delay could give rise to a pot bound condition, which will promote premature flowering and make the roots reluctant to enter the new compost when it is eventually potted on.

STOPPING

Stopping or pinching out is the removal of the growing tip of the young stem using a small pair of scissors, tweezers, or the delicate use of the fingernails. The growing tip should be removed just above the next pair of developing leaves. Essentially there are three reasons for stopping, the first is to create additional growing stems and therefore more flowers. Secondly, to shape the plant and thirdly, to control the time in the season the plant starts to flower. It is a practice that must be adopted for all types of growth and the simple logic behind the removal of the growing tip is that from the new top, at least two stems will start to grow and when in turn they are stopped, they will also produce at least two stems. Thus by a progression of four stops the plant will have a minimum of 16 stems.

Always try to envisage the type of plant that you want - a compact bushy plant or one with a more open structure, the decision should be guided both by the cultivar and your own preference. Making this decision determines whether the plant should be stopped at every pair of leaves for compact growth, or every two or three pairs for a more open structure. Slow growing plants benefit from a relaxed approach, vigorous and wayward cultivars can be restrained by a tighter stopping programme. It is important that the plant is stopped as a whole, rather than in a haphazard fashion, so that the overall shape of the plant can be controlled.

Stopping a plant delays flowering. The length of time from the last stop to flowering depends on the variety, their growing environment, the time of the year, weather conditions and the general well being of the plant. Thus there can be no hard and fast rule, however the following guide lines are useful :-
Singles 7-9 weeks **Doubles 9-11 weeks** **Semi Doubles 8-10 weeks**
Species & Triphyllas 12-14 weeks.

A greater degree of control can be exercised if a written record of stopping dates and the date the plant comes into flower is recorded. Many growers record this information on the plant label, which is used the following year to determine stopping times. It is the penultimate stop, which should be timed to be 2 or 3 weeks before the final stop, which has some effect on the final stopping date

STAKING OR TYING IN

Staking, which is the fastening of the stem to split canes, may be necessary to maintain the all round shape of the plant. A well grown plant should not need to be staked. However some cultivars require staking as a means of support, but all staking must be unobtrusive. As with other aspects of fuchsia growing try and anticipate the ultimate shape and therefore make a decision as early as possible as to whether your plant will need staking. If the answer is yes, then the stakes should be inserted and the ties are in place as soon as possible after the final potting. The reason for this action is to ensure that the plant has time to grow and hide the stakes and ties. A young plant full of flower will often need an emergency tie in - as the weight of flowers will often threaten to damage a whole stem - try and keep it as discreet as possible, so that the eye sees the plant and not the cane.

THE FINAL TOUCHES

You have given your original cuttings many months of tender loving care and looked after their needs of feeding, warmth and light, stopped them, shaped them, kept them pest and disease free. It now makes sense that you bring out the very best in them for the great occasion - whether it be for you own garden, a show, or a display etc.

Let us consider that your plant is going to a fuchsia show - if they have been grown out of doors, they should be brought under cover about 14 days before you want them to be at their best, to protect them from the weather, and to protect the flowers from bees or wasps. When you are satisfied they will be able to be exhibited, consult the show schedule to ensure each plant meets the requirements of the class and fully acquaint yourself with the rules, regulations and conditions which are set out in the schedule. Then submit your entry to the Show Secretary before the deadline. On the day before the show, start to titivate your plant, by wiping away all the accumulation of dirt on the outside of the pot, and give it a polish. Clear away all the debris that has accumulated on the surface of the compost and pick out all the dead leaves and flowers which are trapped by the framework of the stems. Remove all damaged, dead and yellowing leaves that are adhering to the stems, also remove all damaged and decaying flowers, and any seed pods which are still on the plant. Examine the plant to ensure it is clean and disease free. If a few pests are present remove them using a small brush dipped in insecticide, paying special attention to the flowers. Carefully open any full sized buds which are on the point of opening and do not forget an overnight watering.

There are many different ways of getting your plant to the hall and it pays to work out the best method some days before the show. If you are carrying them in a car you can encase them in stockinette, which you can purchase as tubular car cleaning cloths. Cut a length, invert your plant holding it by the pot, in one hand, place the tube over the pot and gradually draw it up and stretch it down to encase the plant. To remove it stretch the cloth at the pot end and draw it off the plant. There are many other ways, such as wrapping your plant in newspaper, or old soft curtain or cutting a pot sized hole in the base of a cardboard box to make the plant secure. All these methods ensure that the branches of the plant do not get entangled with one another during transit. Arrive at the hall with plenty of time to spare to collect your entry cards and to give the plants a final dressing, tease out the blooms which have got lost in the foliage, using a piece of cane (not your fingers). Holding the plant upside down and giving it a gentle shake will often help. Prune off any protruding stakes. Keep calm, look at and learn from the other exhibitors and don't hesitate to seek assistance if you are in any doubt. The stewards are there to help you. One last check ensures that your plants are in the right classes and make them give an impact by not losing them amongst other plants. If necessary place them on top of an upturned pot so that they can be seen, and always place them with their best side forward. Place you entry card in front of your exhibit, name the variety and your job is done.

Allow yourself plenty of time to stage your plants. If you have a lot to stage it is easy to get confused and place them in the wrong class, and often you do not have enough time for the final check. Quite an amount of preparatory work can be done the day before. For example, every plant has one side better than the other, and exhibitors try to make sure that the best side is facing the judge. The best side can be determined the day before, and the plant label is inserted on this side, so when you are staging, make sure the label is pointing the right way. Make a list of the classes you are entering and earmark the plant which you are intending to enter and place a label showing the class number in the pot, to be removed when staging. Remember you have spent a lot of time and effort in getting a plant on the show bench, so make sure it is where it should be and looking it's best. Good luck - it's great fun.

Perhaps reading or skipping over the last few paragraphs you may be thinking that you are not interested in showing your fuchsias - but I am certain that you will want them to look their best whether they are to be in your front garden or entered in a show. The principles are the same, during the flowering season - regular maintenance - removing pods, yellow leaves etc. will ensure a prolonged period of flowers, fine foliage etc.

Enjoy growing fuchsias - they will give you many hours of pleasure right throughout the year!

BASKETS AND HANGING POTS

By D. Boor

To my mind this is one of the most satisfying methods of showing off the beauty of the fuchsia, especially if the more lax, trailing, type of plants are used when one can look up into a mass of cascading flowers and really appreciate their beauty. Some people do however use the more bushy type of plant such as Waveney Gem or Shelford and providing they do fulfil the criteria of covering the whole of the basket can look very attractive, although I personally would consider them more suitable for a raised container.

On the whole baskets are easy to produce, although I think a little more forward planning is required. In some cases a longer growing season may be required (if intending to show) particularly for the larger doubles, where it may be better for showing purposes to use a two year old basket where a harder framework has been developed. This will then more easily support the heavier blooms, rather than pulling apart to display a large hole in the middle of the basket.

If it is possible to obtain young plants or take cuttings in the autumn then you should have excellent plants to plant up in the spring, giving you plenty of time to fully develop the top and side growth needed to cover the container completely. These should ideally have been stopped at least twice and be in a minimum of 9cm (3½") pots. Alternatively you could plant three well rooted cuttings in a 9cm (3½") pot treating them as one plant and then planting the required number of pots into the basket or hanging pot.

The number of plants you will need for each basket will depend on its size. There is no reason why you should not use just one plant but this will take much longer to develop into the size required to make a good hanging basket and may require over wintering. As a rough guide I would suggest four plants for a 30cm (12") diameter container (5 - 6 plants for a 35cm (14") diameter and perhaps 7 for a 40cm (16") one). I always use one plant in the centre of my basket and spread the others evenly around the outside.

There is no reason why one should not use different cultivars but unless you know your plants really well I would preferably use just one cultivar. The reasoning behind this is that different cultivars have differing rates of growth and are likely to flower at different times. A good basket should be a mass of evenly grown foliage with a covering of flowers from the crown of the plants to the ends of the trailing growths.

There are many types of basket available in the shops nowadays - for show purposes the ruling simply states that the diameter should not be more than 40cm (16") and the depth not more than 22.5cm (9"). It should be commercially produced as a hanging basket and should be of open mesh construction. You should also cheek individual show schedules to see if any local restrictions apply. Hanging pots have solid sides and again should be commercially produced as a hanging pot, not be simply ordinary pots with hangers attached to them.

A lining will he needed for the wire baskets - a sheet of polythene is perfectly acceptable providing you insert drainage holes. After all, you are not going to see the basket once your plants have made adequate growth. Be warned however - full sun beating down onto polythene can raise the temperature within the basket quite considerably and this will burn the plant's roots, so I always use a net lining first and then a polythene liner. I always use a peat-based compost with perlite and grit added as this is much lighter to move around. To this I add a long acting food (such as Osmacote). This has a wax coating which melts at 70°F. (20 °C), just the temperature a fuchsia stops growing at, and 1 do not wish my basket to stop growing when I am trying to produce long trailing growths. It is also available as a backup if I forget to give it's normal feed. I tend to avoid using water retaining granules such as "Swell gel" as they tend to push themselves to the top of the compost, holding water on the top and making the young plants more prone to botrytis in the early part of the year - however I do use a fibre mat at the base of the basket which has water retaining granules trapped in the fibres - these are known as 'Fertile Fibre' mats. They hold water at the base of the basket and encourage the root growth to reach down through the compost, acting as a reservoir in summer when I am not always around to give the frequent watering required.

To make up your basket, stand it in a large bucket or pot for ease of filling. Pour in a quantity of compost - approx 2.5cm (1") - place in the fibre mat then place in about another 5cm (2") of compost. Get some pots of the same size as the ones your plants are already growing in and arrange them in their positions with one in the middle and the rest around the outside. Fill in the baskets and pots with compost A tap on the bench will settle the compost, then it will be possible to remove the empty pots and replace them with the plants from the growing pots. They will hardly know they have been moved. I personally leave the middle pot empty in place for a further month, keeping my extra plant by the side ready to be planted in the middle. During the time I am waiting to plant the centre plant I give it one feed of a higher potash content to encourage a slightly woodier framework, which will be pinched as a bush and will not then pull apart at a later date.

The earlier in the year you make up your basket the better, but you must not be tempted to place it outside until all risk of frost has passed, usually the end of May. During this time the biggest risk to growth is the likelihood of the plant growth developing botrytis so be careful not to over water - the roots are not yet that well developed and could easily be drowned. Try and ensure good air movement through the developing growth (another reason for leaving out the centre plant initially) and make sure that any leaves that do drop are immediately removed.

Whilst the plants are continuing to grow they need frequent "pinching out" of the growing shoots each time two or three sets of leaves have formed. This encourages bushy growth, which will soon fill the top of the basket and trail over the sides. A half basket, sometimes called a wall basket, is ideal for breaking up a bare wall, fence or trellis. The same method is used and it will be necessary to have three or four plants around the side and one in the middle.

Hanging pots can be just as attractive, but being smaller may be more manageable. They range in size from 15cm (6") to 25cm (10"). A 15cm (6”) one will probably only need one plant

Feeding should be carried out on a regular basis. I use a balanced feed, at quarter strength, at least once a day. I way have to water two or three times a day during hot spells, so only one of these needs to contain feed - but this can quickly be lost with frequent watering.

I have suggested growing fuchsias only here, top planted only - this is preferable if you intend to show your fuchsias, and the public do love seeing a well-grown basket. However there is no reason of course why they cannot be planted up with other hanging plants, both flowering and foliage, to give a truly magnificent display. Keep removing the dead flowers and seedpods, continue to feed regularly and they will provide you with flowers for a whole season. I have had a single basket in flower continuously from May until November - cheap for the price, and the envy of all the neighbours.

STANDARDS

By A. Phillips

Growing a standard fuchsia seems to set the average grower insurmountable problems. This being the second most popular question at any information table. With this article I will try to dispel some of the problems of growing a standard.

Any fuchsia cultivar can be trained as a standard, and my first reaction when obtaining a new cultivar is to run it up as a standard. But for the first time grower, it would pay to select one of the easier cultivars to start with. A selection of these can be found at the end of the article.

To grow a full or half standard for the show bench you ideally need a heated greenhouse. Mini, quarter and the smaller half standards can be run up in one season. For either form of cultivation cuttings need to be taken in the early spring, February or March. Cutting material ideally needs to be young, fresh, healthy and even in growth. Look for cutting material where the leaf size is the same on either side of the stem. Some schools of thought recommend looking for cuttings with triformation leaves, but again ensure even sized leaves. Take and root your cuttings as you would normally. I use ordinary potting compost 80% to Perlite 20% measured by volume, mixed well together, ensuring all lumps are removed, moisten so that when squeezed in your hand the mix just holds together. Put the mix into your preferred container, and I find used margarine tubs with a few holes made in the bottom for drainage to be ideal. Place the selected cuttings in the container ensuring no plant material is touching, and place the full container on a heated bed to give bottom heat of around 15°C (60°F), but do not cover the tops. When the cuttings are rooted, let them grow on in the cutting container, off the heated bed for about 7-10 days. Select the cuttings showing the signs of the most vigour, and of even growth, pot on into the smallest pot it will fit into, and add a small split cane, **a)** to give support, **b)** to prevent the tendency to nip out the tip of a potential standard for cutting material.

As your plant grows keep it potted on. ***It is essential never to allow a standard to become pot bound while running up the stem.*** Potting on in half inch pot sizes every time. As the height increases keep your support always above the top of the embryo standard. Tie the stem loosely to the cane. For this, strips of ladies tights or stockings are an excellent medium, as this material stretches to allow the swelling of the young plant's stem without the dangers of cutting into the stem as some wire reinforced ties do if not checked regularly. With the upward progress of the plant, remove all the side shoots, except for the two pairs immediately

below the growing tip. These are left on as insurance in case the growing tip is accidentally damaged, if this happens with two sets of sideshoots a head can be formed even if the desired height has not been achieved. ***Under no circumstances ever remove the leaves from the stem.*** The leaves are the lungs of the plant, and are also used to develop the necessary sugars to give health and vigour to the stem.
At all stages of the plants life to keep growth even and it is most important that you do with a standard, turn daily by a quarter turn each day. If this is not done when running up the stem, then you will find that your stem will develop nasty twists.

If you are growing your standard on through summer to flower the next year, then it is essential that you keep the plant in vegetative growth by feeding high nitrogen feed at each watering.

When your standard has reached the required height, and if you intend to show the plant, measurement is from the top of the compost to the first branch, but remember after you make your stop of the growing tip, the length of stem will elongate slightly, so never stop to the maximum size. When coming up to the time of stopping the upward growth, I ensure that I have a minimum of four sets of side shoots from which to form the head. When I remove the lead shoot, I always aim to stop at least the top two sets of side shoots. I then form the head by treating it as a "bush on a stick" and stop at every two/ three sets of leaves as the head starts to form, stopping each tip at the same time.

If you grow your plant on in vegetative growth through the winter, it is essential that you keep your heat in balance with the light. In the winter the level of light is so low, that if your plant is kept in temperatures in excess of 5°C (40°F). you are in danger of getting long jointed weak growth, and this is not what is required of a good standard. Slow close jointed growth in the winter months gives a good, strong, thick stem. Also remember, that the floor of a greenhouse is the coldest part, and standards usually stand on the floor. Lift your standard up by placing it on an upturned pot, I try to use 22.5cm (9") ones as this lifts the root ball into nice warm air.

Standards are usually difficult to overwinter if you do not have a heated greenhouse, but anywere they can be stored frost free will suffice, dry out slightly and completely defoliate, raise the pot and wrap with horticultural fleece, one layer is recommended to give five degrees of protection, so two or three layers should be adequate. Protect the stem with a suitable sized piece of pipe insulation. the split foam type is ideal and the thicker walled the better, then drape the whole lot with fleece. Inspect at regular intervals and never allow to dry out completely.

A few good varieties to begin with are: Celia Smedley. Snowcap. Barbara, Checkerboard. Display. Shelford. Rufus. Annabel. and Dollar Princess. For Mini Standards, use smaller flowered varieties such as any of the Thumbs.

TRAINED SHAPES

By G. Oke

Fuchsias are probably one of the most versatile plants that we can grow. Besides being grown as bush or shrub plants either in pots or the open garden and trained to produce standards, baskets or hanging pots, they can be trained or shaped into many other forms by simple clipping/pruning or tying. However, this does not apply to every cultivar that is available to us. Some cultivars will not be suitable simply because they are either very vigorous, become too woody or are long jointed.

The training of any fuchsia to your own requirements needs a degree of skill and patience. However, when attempting to train a fuchsia into other shapes it does require a higher degree of skill which you will acquire from experience, plenty of time, patience and diligence to be successful. Training fuchsias into your desired shape can be a very rewarding and satisfying hobby, you will need to experiment with different shapes and with different cultivars until you find the formula that suits you. It may take you several attempts or even years to grow a specimen shape, but the thrill of one's achievement is difficult to put into words.

When deciding on what shape you would like to achieve you firstly have to make or purchase a frame on which to grow your plants these can be made using canes, garden wire (plastic coated is best) or any material which can be covered without being seen.

Selecting the cultivar which you wish to train should be done as early in the Spring as possible. They should be healthy unstopped plants ideally in 5cm (2") or 9cm (3½") pots that have not started to ripen as they need to have pliable stems and branches to allow them to be bent/placed around/to the frame. The stem and branches are held in place using strips of nylon which if not tied too tightly allows the plants to grow without restricting their growth. They could also be platted. Care must be taken or Botrytis will set into the growth where it has been tied in. This can be avoided by keeping your plants well ventilated by either opening the greenhouse door(s) or by using fans to improve air circulation.

PYRAMIDS and CONICALS

A pyramid has a square or triangular base and triangular sides of equal proportion meeting at the top. The width at the base should be in balance with its height i.e 0.9m (3 feet) high could have a base approximately 0.45m (1.5 feet).
A conical has a circular base and tapering sides, giving the effect of a tall tapering tree.The width at the base should be in balance with its height i.e. 0.9m

(3feet) high could have a base approximately 30cm (1 foot) in diameter. They can be grown using one or more plants to obtain the effect of either a pyramid or conical and size is not restricted other than by the space available for over wintering or by transport should you wish to exhibit your plants.

Growing such shapes is without doubt one of the most difficult and will be a test of any growers skill. I think it will take two or three years to grow and form these types of shape and it will require constant attention to keep it in good shape. It will require turning and feeding regularly. I am sure you will need to grow it through the winter in leaf in a heated greenhouse or conservatory.

When selecting your plant(s) they need to be unstopped and grown on into 9cm (3½") or maybe 11cm (4½") pots and allowed to run upto 22.5cm/ 25cm (9"/10") in height before stopping. Once stopped choose the strongest of the two top laterals which becomes your new leader, which should be tied in place. The side branches are tied in place and stopped to fill in the sides. It is important that you alternate the stopping of the leading tip (first), then the side branches and then the tip. This process is continued until the plant(s) reach your chosen height and the shape can be clearly identified when viewed from all sides.

PILLARS and COLUMNS.

A pillar or column should form a cylindrical shape from top to bottom when viewed from all sides. The graceful pillar or column should be fully covered with healthy foliage and flower and may be supported by a single stake. They can be produced by using one or more plants, it is better to use all the same cultivar as they will produce the same type of growth patterns and flowering times.

The methods used to achieve these shapes are identical as for growing a pyramid or conical. Except the growth should be equal diameter from top to bottom.

Some varieties which may be used for these shapes are :-
Lye's Unique, Kolding Perle, Border Queen, Charming, Baby Bright, Caradela, Sylvia Barker, Waveney Gem, Janice Ann, Ernie Bromley, Linda Grace.

The list could go on and on, but the best way is to select a cultivar which you like and have a go and enjoy the challenge.

ESPALIERS and FANS

To obtain these shapes plants are trained on a lattice or frame. Espaliers have horizontally trained branches and should be of equal length, with the branches matched symmetrically on both sides of the centre stem of the plant or exhibit for its full height. The height and width of the espalier should be of good proportion to the size of the pot and present a balanced plant or exhibit when viewed from the front. Fans should have branches trained into the shape of a fan. They should be trained to give a visual balance when viewed from the front with equal growth on both sides of an imaginary centre line.

These shapes can be grown using one or more plants, for the best results it is best to use the same cultivar(s).

To grow an espalier, it is usual to have four parallel sets of horizontal branches on each side of the stem. When selecting your plant(s) for this type of training they should have eight pairs of leaves, before it is stopped. Having selected which four branches you wish to train, they are tied to the frame at right angles from the centre stem using a soft tie (nylon tights) and allowed to grow until the required length is reached. The other four branches which are at right angles to those used should be removed so a flat back is obtained. When the branches have reached your chosen width they should be stopped to allow the side shoots to develop, these should be stopped at every pair of leaves. All new branches should be tied in as soon as possible. It will be necessary to pull some of the leaves through from the back of the structure to cover the frame work.

To grow a fan, it is usual to select a plant which is a strong growing cultivar, and allow it to develop four pairs of of leaves, before removing the growing tip. Fuchsias are of a cruciform shape and when stopped the pairs of branches grow at right angles to one another. As the plant (s) are being trained to lie flat on a frame /structure, it is necessary to remove either the first and third pair of branches, or the second and fourth pairs as soon as they are forming. If more then one plant is used we should stop one plant at the first and third and the other at the second and fourth branches. We are left with four or eight branches which are tied to our frame/structure as they develop. When tying in the branches it is important that they are tied equally from the centre line of the plant(s) to form the shape of a fan, the angle of the branches to the pot need not be at 90 degrees to achieve the desired fan shape. When each side branch has developed another two pairs of leaves, they should be stopped again. From the resulting growth select the two which are growing in the same direction as the frame and tie in and remove the other two. This process is continued until the desired size is obtained. It is possible in the early stages of training to use a piece of card on the back of the frame to encourage the plant(s) to grow towards the front only. To obtain a good shaped fan the plant(s) should be grown on slowly through the winter. If it is not possible and the plant(s) have to be rested, it is best if they are laid flat, to prevent the sap from falling.

Some varieties which may be used for these shapes are :-
Border Queen, Baby Bright, Caradela, Sylvia Barker, Waveney Gem, Janice Ann, Ernie Bromley, Linda Grace, Miss California, Swingtime, Fascination, Golden Marinka, Marinka

CIRCLES, DOUBLE CIRCLES, FIGURE OF EIGHT OR CROWNS.

These shapes are obtained by training one or more plants around a strong wire shaped to your choice i.e. single circle or double circle where the second circle is positioned at right angles to the first circle. The best type of plants to use for these shapes are those which produce soft thin wiry growth i.e. some of the basket cultivars or the Encliandras, but be careful they are not too vigorous for the size of frame which should be in proportion to the size of pot. To grow a single circle select a plant and stop at the first pair of leaves and tie each branch as they develop to the frame or use two plants and plant them so they cross each other and tie them to the frame. Allow the branches or plants to develop without removing the growing tip until they have met in the middle. It is important to tie the side branches into the frame or if possible plat the branches to obtain the circle shape and keep it even around the entire shape. For a double circle the plant is stopped at two pairs of leaves or where four plants are used, then use the same method as a single ring. A figure of eight is just two rings on top of each other so instead of stopping the plants when they meet you simply continue growing them onto the top circle using the same method as before. The crown is simply a ring on its side and may consist of two rings joined together using short pieces of wire to obtain the desired effect.

OTHER TRAINED SHAPES

Today it is possible to purchase many frames already bent to a given shape, such as Rabbits, Squirrels, Cats, Dogs, Teddy Bears etc., but you can let your own imagination run riot. To train or shape your plant(s) into your chosen design follow the same steps as for Rings etc. You may like to take your plants just around the frame work or even try to fill in the centre, but be careful, the sharper the bend in the stem required to obtain your shape the higher the risk of botrytis or the likely hood of disease setting in.

There are other designs which require training, some that I have seen are :-
Helicopter - grown using two different cultivars as standards in the same pot, only one is stopped before the other.
Spiral or Helter Skelter - grown on a frame using one or two different cultivars using a similar technique as for rings etc.
Decorative standards - two or more plants grown in one pot with their stems platted or twisted around each other.

Some varieties which may be used for these shapes are :-
Waveney Gem, Cambridge Louie, Sylvia Barker, Linda Grace, Fairy Floss, Radings Karin, Karen Isles, Ariel, Jiddles, Miniature Jewels, Lottie Hobby.

There are many more cultivars which you could try. The best way is to try different cultivars and see how well you do, but remember it takes time and patience.

SMALL POT CULTURE

It is often confusing when you read a show schedule and you see a class for small pot culture. What this really means is a plant(s) that have been trained into a recognisable shape other than as a BUSH or SHRUB in a 13cm (5¼") pot. It is not the intention to grow the largest trained shape in the smallest pot, but to ensure the frame/structure and plants are in proportion to the size of pot. Also available in this class is a 15cm (6") basket, many use a flour sieve with the handle removed, the growing technique is the same as for baskets or hanging pots only in miniature.

It is possible to grow any of the shapes mentioned in the training section for the small pot culture class in our shows.

Mini standards or table standards as they are sometimes called, although grown in a 13cm (5¼") pot are not exhibited in the small pot culture class. The best type of cultivars for this type of training are the ones with small leaves and flowers or many of the Encliandra types.

CLIMBERS

The term climber is perhaps misleading for fuchsias, as fuchsias are not truly a climbing plant.

You might however have a part of a greenhouse or conservatory where you would like to try growing a plant(s) to provide you with some shade as well as colour. The plant(s) should be planted in the border of your greenhouse or conservatory and trained up to the desired height, removing the side shoots as the plant develops. When your plant(s) has reached the height required let three pairs of side shoots develop and grow before removing the growing tip. The side shoots are then tied to the rafters or wires in the roof and they will eventually form a canopy. As the side shoots develop you will need to stop some of them as they develop to encourage the plant(s) to thicken up and produce an abundance of foliage and flower.

Although you heat your greenhouse or conservatory in winter it is best to give some added protection to the stem and canopy. The stem can be protected using foam strips of pipe lagging and the canopy by placing horticultural fleece between the top of the plant(s) canopy and the glass.

I would suggest that you use some of our known hardies for this type of growth or just experiment with a cultivar you enjoy.

AFTER CARE

Before you start to grow fuchsias into trained shapes the question you have to ask yourself is - What am I going to do with it when I've grown it? For example, Will it fit through my greenhouse door? Can I overwinter it easily? Believe me, if you successfully grow a well trained shape you will want to show it off either in your garden or at a show. Yes, some shapes take up less room than others, so please think carefully before you start growing as you will spend a lot of time and require a lot of patience to achieve the finished shape, but it will be worth the effort.

Remember your plant(s) will need to be kept free of frost and cold drafts in the winter months. If you have large shapes don't stand them directly on the floor put them up by about a 30cm (12"). If you do have them on the bench remember to turn them so they grow evenly (it's the part furthest away from the glass that will grow most) not the side nearest the glass. To keep the sap in the stems you may need to lay the plant(s) down on its side or flat, but keep them off the floor.

To prepare your plant(s) for the winter make sure they are under cover in early to mid Autumn and stop watering them until the leaves droop. Don't be too eager, wait a few more days, and then start to reduce the size of the plant(s) by cutting back all of the current years growth to one pair of eyes, remember to maintain the desired shape. The cut ends should now be sealed to prevent fungus from entering the wound. To do this you can use "Copydex", or hormone rooting powder, which contains a fungicide. Dip the wound in the powder or paint the wound with a little "Copydex". Remember when watering not to over do it and its best to wait for a couple of days after pruning. Remove any leaves which are still attached and spray your plant(s) with a fungicide such as Dithane, Benlate or Hexyl plus. Also keep an eye on your plant for signs of attack from vine weevil during the Winter period.

Apart from frost, sunshine can cause damage to our plant(s) in the early part of the year. A few hours of sunshine will dry out the stems and induce die back, so cover them with fleece or newspaper, until growth can be seen.

Another problem that can occur when spraying your dormant plant(s) occasionally to keep the wood soft, and to encourage new growth is Botrytis. To prevent it spray when there is plenty of air movement and keep the greenhouse well ventilated, so the water can dry off and not leave the wood too wet for long periods. A precaution which can be used is to spray using Benlate on a couple of occasions. Care must be taken with the young new growth as aphids and whitefly can be found in early Spring. If you use an insecticide to control them do not use it at full strength as it could damage the new delicate foliage, especially if the plant remains wet for some time. So ventilate your greenhouse and use the insecticide at half strength.

Also remember these plants will not go on indefinitely and you will need to be growing them on and starting new ones every year to avoid missing a year.

MULTI-PLANT CULTIVATION.

By Arthur Phillips

Multiple plant growing has been around the fuchsia scene for a very long time, used especially when growing baskets, hanging pots and tubs. Cuttings of the same cultivar are grown on in pots until they become well established plants, then four or five of them are placed together into the larger container and grown on. Professional nurseries have also been using the same technique, planting three or four plants of the same cultivar into a large pot to produce a big plant in a shorter time.

However, although the Multi-Plant method described below has the same affect, it produces a bigger plant in a shorter time, it is achieved differently. Follow these methods and for some inexplicable reason the plants behave differently.

The secret to the success of Multi-Planting fuchsias starts at the very beginning, at the time the cuttings are taken, and how they are taken and planted. The cuttings need to be just the tip of the shoot and one pair of leaves, the leaves held together just over the growing tip and the ends cropped off to reduce leaf area. Select the cuttings so that they are all about the same size, and are evenly balanced. Take your cutting mix, personally I use ordinary potting compost 80%, and Perlite 20% by volume, well mixed together with all of the large lumps removed. The compost should be just moist (when squeezed in your hand it should just hold together), if it is a bit on the dry side just add water until the required moisture content is achieved, and put your mix into a pot - a 9cm (3½") half pot is ideal for me. Gently settle the compost into the pot, then place the cuttings around the outer edge of the pot, finger width apart. This should give you seven cuttings around. I also place one in the middle.

Place the pot in a suitable place where it can get light without getting scorched by the sun, and leave to root. Do not use bottom heat and do not over water. You can cover the top with a plastic bag with a small hole cut in the top or a proprietary propagating lid, but I prefer rooting my Multi-Plants without covering them.

When the cuttings have rooted, bring the complete pot onto the bench and grow them on together, stopping it and potting it on as one plant. The major difference you will notice is that the plants develop a fibrous root system and there are no large taproots being grown. This has the advantage of getting more top growth from minimal root growth, result a bigger plant in a smaller pot.

There are a few points to this growth method that you should note. Firstly, be very careful with the watering especially in the early days after rooting has taken place. Rooting cuttings, even in a half pot, can result in the compost at the bottom becoming over watered and becoming sour. Only water when the compost is starting to dry out, the best check is the weight of the pot- a light pot means the need for water. When you do need to water always dribble it in from the top of the pot, and never in excess. Secondly the plants must be kept scrupulously clean, always remove debris as soon as it occurs, dead plant matter in such a densely planted container leads to Botrytis. Like wise ensure that the leaves in the early days are not touching, this again could lead to Botrytis. This method may not seem easy in the first instance but with a few slight changes to your cultural technique it soon becomes as easy to manage as one plant in a pot. Once you become proficient at growing fuchsias you will find that it is much easier and quicker to grow large, beautifully shaped plants

The Multi-Plant method, again for inexplicable reasons, has some differing effects on plants grown this way. The more vigorous long jointed cultivars such as "Checkerboard" grow as a more compact plant. This should have the effect, if the method is used properly, of eventually bringing some of these types of plant and especially the long jointed, slow growing double cultivars back to the showbench. This method, because of the reduced number of stops, gives a more open growth form.

Do not be surprised to see differences in growth, foliage or even flower size on some cultivars. And if you do, do not think that the changes have occurred because you are growing several in a pot and that they are being dwarfed in some way. The reason for the change is simply because of the different root system Some advantages of multi planting fuchsias, as opposed to growing a single plant in a pot, are:- **a)** Cuttings taken in early Spring will make substantial flowering plants in the same season. **b)** Pot grown plants do not flush flower, they flower almost continuously for month after month. **c)** Plants have a more natural habit of growth. **d)** Different types of cultivar can now be grown together in the same pot, even doubles and singles grow at the same rate and come into flower together, although stopped at the same time.

Most Cultivars and Species are suitable for this method of cultivation, but the more vigorous long jointed cultivars, especially the double flowered ones benefit most. There are several excellent publications available which cover this method of cultivation in more detail and for anyone interested I would strongly recommend reading one of these.

GROWING TRIPHYLLAS.

By Paul Heavens

Many of the plants that are popularly known today as the triphylla hybrids were raised in Germany at the turn of the century. *F. triphylia, F. fulgens* and *F. boliviana* all played a part in the early development of these hybrids but it is by no means certain that *F. triphylla* was in the parentage of all these early crosses, therefore triphylla hybrid tends to be accepted as a descriptive rather than accurate term. As a group, they tend to have a much more open type of growth and many develop their flowers on a drooping type of flowering stem. Once they come into flower they will flower continuously for a very long period. The flowers are primarily in the scarlet orange colour range although this is broadening thanks to the hybridisers, the tube tends to be much longer than the sepals, and the petals are small.

In recent years many new cultivars have been introduced and this has helped to broaden the colour range to include pale pinks and aubergine shades. There is also a white flowered triphylla named OUR TED which is most attractive but can be challenging to grow.

The triphylla types are extremely adaptable and relatively easy group of fuchsias to grow. Whether your interests lie in exhibiting, summer bedding, or in pots or containers for garden decoration, you will find many plants in this group ideal for your requirements. One of the advantages of the triphylla types is that they tend to be more tolerant of direct sunlight and higher temperatures than the normal fuchsias. This makes them of great value in situations such as conservatories, south facing borders and tubs on sunny patios.
Unfortunately they are not as hardy as most other fuchsias and will seldom survive the winter outdoors. However strong young plants can be bedded out after all the risk of frost has passed, and they will flower continually until the first frosts of Autumn.

BEDDING OUT.

If they are to flower well, a site where they will receive a reasonable amount of sunlight should be chosen. Although they will stand full sun, the ideal site offers morning sun and some shade during the hottest part of the afternoon. The planting hole should be well prepared, and if your garden soil is not of a good quality, you should add a handful or two of garden compost to improve the soil structure. Select well grown vigorous upright cultivars from four or five inch pots, and set the plant in the planting hole so that it is approximately two inches lower than it was in the pot. Water the plant, and continue to water regularly until well established. Remember, do not plant out until all risk of frost has passed.

POTS AND CONTAINERS.

By planting in pots and other containers you are able to increase the variety of cultivars that you grow, plants with a lax or trailing habit will not show themselves well in the garden border. Young plants should be potted on regularly and not allowed to become pot bound. When potting on, increase the pot sizes in gradual stages, never go straight from a small pot to a large one, as this will result in an excessive quantities of compost around the roots, which can become waterlogged very easily.
When planting up large containers such as patio tubs, select cultivars which are vigorous or alternatively plant three of the same variety together, both upright and lax types are recommended for best effect. Some cultivars are best suited for growing in hanging containers, and with careful choice it is possible to grow very fine baskets, and wall baskets.
Cultivars which do not respond well to stopping, or those that are less vigorous are best planted in six or eight inch hanging pots.

GROWING FOR THE SHOW BENCH.

The introduction of classes for smaller triphyllas in 9cm (3½") pots has made the exhibiting of these plants open to all. No longer do you need to heat a greenhouse overwinter to be able to show (and win) in a triphylla class. Plants for this class can be grown in much the same way that you would grow any other fuchsia, however, the choice of cultivar becomes more important because you will need to select the less vigorous types with a compact habit of growth. Suggested cultivars might include ADINDA, MANDI or SOPHIE'S SUPRIZE all of which have proved themselves suitable.

Many growers have difficulty producing high quality large triphyllas for exhibition. Most of the triphyllas are not free branching, and can be prone to a yellowing and dropping of the lower leaves. This means that you may need to give them a slightly different treatment if you are to achieve a really bushy plant. Slightly longer cuttings than normal are required, and the lower leaves are removed, so that two or three leaf nodes can be inserted below the level of the compost. When removing the lower leaves ensure that you do not damage the dormant bud in the leaf axil. Hopefully these buds will develop and appear as shoots from below the soil surface. It is these shoots arising from below soil level which will help to increase the bushiness of the plant. Some cultivars will produce these sub surface shoots more readily than others, and it is these that make the finest show plants.

Cuttings will root at any time of the year, but those taken in Spring root most quickly and produce the strongest young plants. When the cuttings have rooted, they should be potted up into small pots keeping the young plant as low as possible in the compost. As the plant develops, it should be potted into the next size as soon as the roots are seen to be running around the edge of the soil ball. Again all effort should be made to get the plant as low as possible. Only a very small amount of compost should be placed into the base of the new pot, the bulk of it should go onto the surface so that more of the plant's stems are buried. This will have two effects, firstly it helps to compensate for any leaves which may have been lost from the base, secondly by burying the branches deeper you will encourage even more shoots from below soil level. All subsequent potting on should follow this method.
Good results can be achieved by stopping the plant at every third pair of leaves, triphylla types should not be stopped too tightly in the latter stages as this will result in small leaves and an overall stunted appearance. An alternative method of stopping which has proved to be very effective is to stop the plants at one pair of leaves for the first stop, two pairs at the second stop and three pairs thereafter. This second method produces plants with a better overall shape, but they do tend to be slightly smaller.

During the first season of the plant's life I concentrate on building up a good framework to the plant with as many shoots as possible arising from below the soil surface. I do not worry too much about the overall appearance of the plant as I will not be exhibiting it in it's first season. By late summer of the first year your plant will probably be in a five or six inch pot and will need cutting back. (See overwintering). In the Spring, once the plants are growing well, and depending on the size of the plant, remove one or two inches of compost from the bottom of the root ball using a sharp knife (a serrated bread knife is ideal). Then by rubbing a little of the compost from the side of the root ball, it should be possible to drop the plant back into the pot, but lower down. Any new compost can then be placed in the top of the pot, thereby burying more branches and encouraging more basal shoots. Whether plastic or clay pots are used is a matter of preference, but the larger triphyllas do seem to grow and perform better in clays and I would recommend this type once plants are above the six inch pot stage.

The final stopping date for show purposes is approximately twelve to fifteen weeks, with the true terminal flowering types requiring the latter.

OVERWINTERING.

Plants should be reduced in height by approximately one third and given protection from frost. They can be safely overwintered in a dormant state at a minimum temperature of thirty five degrees Fahrenheit (two Celsius). The compost must be kept just moist, never wet. It is not essential for plants overwintered by this method to have light, so a garage or frost free shed would suffice. In Spring cut the plants back to within two or three inches of the soil surface and place in a light position, and as soon as the new growth starts to appear, a weak feed of high nitrogen fertilizer is recommended. For those wishing to grow very large plants for exhibition, cut back to within three or four inches of the soil surface in late summer, then lay the plants on their side in a shady position outside. By laying the plants down in this way you will help to encourage new shoots to be formed low down and not just at the branch tips. Spray the old wood each day as this will help to keep it soft and produce more shoots. As the growth appears, it will bend towards the light, it is beneficial to turn the pots every few days. When the plants have a good covering of new growth about one inch long, they can be stood upright.
It is important to move the plants into a greenhouse before the night temperature becomes too low, usually in early Autumn. If the conditions have been correct, it should be possible to give each of the growing tips a stop before the onset of winter. The plants must be kept in good light with a minimum temperature of 40°F (5°C) and kept lightly watered. Feed occasionally with a weak high nitrogen Fertiliser, but be careful not to let the shoots become too leggy. This will happen if the temperature is too high and you are heavy handed with the feed.

COMPOST.

Composts are very much a matter of personal preference, some growers use a soil based compost, and others (the majority these days) use a peat based growing medium. My preference would be to use a peat based compost, but it is most important that it is open and free draining, and that usually requires the addition of extra grit or Perlite at up to twenty per cent, by volume.

FEEDING

In the early part of the season, young plants should be fed regularly with a fertilizer that is high in nitrogen to encourage rapid and healthy growth. In late Spring and for the remainder of the year, switch to a balanced feed. Continuing with a high nitrogenous one would result in long jointed leggy growth.
If you live in a hard water area (high pH), the plants will benefit by being given occasional feeds with a fertilizer containing extra iron such as Maxicrop plus Iron. My feeding regime for show plants is as follows :- Each day the plants are fed with Chempak Liquid Feed at a quarter strength. (Chempak No 2 (High nitrogen) and No 3 (Balanced). Once a week I use Maxicrop Plus Iron in place of the Chempak. It is not usually necessary to feed triphylla types with high potash fertilisers and it is possible that using them may be one of the factors involved in the bottom leaves becoming discoloured and dropping off.

THE FUCHSIA SPECIES

By Jack Lamb

Species of fuchsia are found in the Andes of South America from Venezuela and Colombia to the southern tip at Tierra del Fuego, the south east coastal mountains of Brazil, Haiti, Dominican Republic, the mountains of Mexico, central America, New Zealand and Tahiti.

The recent revision of genus fuchsia by Paul E. Berry, Dennis E. Breedlove, Peter H. Raven and others, has identified and recorded a total of 105 species in the genus. With such a large number it has been necessary to split them into sections, using their physical appearance and geological location. Even so, the very large number that remain in section Fuchsia, has necessitated a grouping of plants, which have similar characteristics.

In the sections Quelusia and Encliandra, there is a slight physical difference between examples within a species. These differences are not great enough to make them a separate botanical species, and within certain species, sub species (ssp) are used to identify plants having these differences.

Section.	Distribution	No. of Species
1. Quelusia	SE Coastal Brazil, Chile and Argentina	9
2. Fuchsia	Tropical Andes, Haiti and Dominican Republic	63
3. Ellobium	Mexico and Central America	3
4. Hemsleyella	Tropical Andes	15
5. Kierschlegeria	Central coastal Chile	1
6. Schufla	Mexico and Central America	2
7. Jiinenezia	Panama and Costa Rica	1
8. Encliandra	Mexico and Central America	6
9. Skinera	New Zealand and Tahiti	3
10. Pachyrrhiza	Peruvian Andes	1
11. Procumbentes	New Zealand	1

1.QUELUSIA. These are found in Southem Andes and in the uplands of S. E. Brazil. Species and sub species within this section are.-

F. alpestris *
F. bracelinae
*F. brovilobis**
*F. compos-portoi**
F. coccinea *
*F. glazioviana**
*F. hatschbachii**
*F. magellanica**
F. regia *
*ssp regia**
*ssp serrae**
*ssp reitzii**

F. coccinea was the first species within the Quelusia section to be grown in England (1788) followed by *F. magellanica* (1821) and *F. regia* (1839) these three were extensively used as parents for the modern day fuchsia.

2. FUCHSIA. These are to be found in the cloud forests of tropical Bolivia, Peru, Ecuador, Columbia. Two species are found in Haiti and Dominican Republic

F. decumata Group

F. fontinalis
F. decussata
F. feneyae
*F. sanctae rosae**

F. loxensis Group

F. scabriuscula
F. loxensis *
F. steyermarkii
F. summa

F.macrophylla Group

F. pilosa
F. macropetala
F. ovalis
F. macrophylla

F. nigricans Group

F. nigricans
*F. pallescens**
*F. sylvatica**
*F. orientalis**
F. glaberima

F. putumayensis Group

*F. putumayensis**
F. cuatrecasii
F. lehmannii
*F. andrei**
F. abrupter

F. petiolaris Group

F. petiolaris *
F. caucana
F. corollata
*F. ampliata**
F. vulcanica *
*F. ayavacensis**

F. venusta Group

*F. gehrigeri**
*F. venusta**
F. scherffiana
F. llewelynii
*F. rivularis**
ssp. pubescens
F. confertiflolia
*F. campii**

F. denticulata Group

*F. magdalanae**
*F. macrostigma**
F. harlingii
*F. denticulata**
*F. austromontana**
F. cochabambana

F. tineta Group

F. tincta
*F. vargasiana**
*F. furfuracea**

F. simplicicaulis Group

F. sanmartina
F. ceracea
*F. simplicicaulis**
F. coriaciflolia

F. sessilifolia Group

*F. sessilifolia**
F. polyantha

F. boliviana Group

*F. wurdackii**
*F. mathewsii**
F. corymbiflora
*F. boliviana**

F. dependens Group	**Not Grouped**
F. hartwegii *	*F. triphylla* *
*F.crassistipula**	*F. pringsheimii**
F. hirtella	*F. verucosa**
F. canescens	
*F. dependens**	
F. cinerea *	

Only *F. boliviana* and *F. triphylla* played an important part in the development of the modern day fuchsia.

3. ELOBIUM. This section covers plants which are endemic to Mexico and Central America. *F. fulgens* is tuberous rooted.

F. splendens * *F. fulgens* * *F. decidua*

Both *F. fulgens* and *F. splendens* played a very important part in the development of the modern day fuchsia.

4. HEMSLEYELLA. A very distinctive group of apetalous species from the Tropical Andes. (Apetalous means without petals)

*F. apetala**	*F. tunariensis*	*F. salicifolia*
*F. juntasensis**	*F. nana**	*F. huanucoensis*
*F. inflata**	*F. chloroloba*	*F. membranacea*
*F. pilaloensis**	*F. insignis**	*F. tillettiana**
F. garleppiana	*F. cestroides*	*F. mezae*

5. KIERSCHLEGERIA. There is only one species within the section, it comes from the hot and desert of Central Chile.

*F. lycioides**

There are a number of hybrids between *F. lycioides* and *F. magellanica* which do cause confusion in this section. The most common is called Fuchsia Rosea, it is often sold in nurseries as *F. lycioides*. Other hybrids carry local native indian names like Thilco, Chilco, Chilio etc. Some of which are hardy in the United Kingdom.

6. SCHUFIA. A distinct section of plants coming from Mexico and Central America. They are easily recognised by their sprays of flowers which resemble the flowers of Lilac.

*F. arborescens**	*F. paniculata**
*ssp. mixensis**	*ssp. paniculata*

7. JIMENEZIA. Found scattered in wet evergreen cloud forests of Costa Rica and Panama

F. jiminezii *

8. ENCLIANDRA. Mexico and Central America. Within this section there is a lot of confusion in naming and the hybrids have superseded the original species. There are also a number of sub species.

*F. microphylla**	*F. encliandra**	*F. thymifolia*
*ssp. aprica**	*ssp. encliandra**	*ssp. minimiflora**
ssp. chiapensis	*ssp. microphylloides*	*ssp. thymifolia**
*ssp. hemsleyana**	*ssp. tetradactyla**	*F. obconica**
*ssp. hidalgensis**	*F. cylindracea**	*F. ravenii**
*ssp. microphylla**		
*ssp quercetorum**		

9. SKINNERA. Two species from New Zealand and one from Tahiti form this group, which are thought to be the oldest plants in the evolution of the fuchsia.

*F. excorticata** *F. perscandens** *F. cyrtandroides**

10. PACHYRRHIZA. A single species from Peru. It has a potato like root system and is very difficult to grow and flower.

F. pachyrriza *

11. PROCUMBENTES. From recent study *F. procumbens* was given its own section because of so many botanical differences with species within its former group SKINNERA.

F. procumbens *

* In cultivation in Europe

INTER-SPECIFIC HYBRIDS

A cross between two separate species is termed an inter-specific hybrid. There are many examples where two species have produced natural hybrids, and there are, of course, a large number that owe their origins to the interference of man. Some of the natural hybrids were considered to be true species by the earlier botanists, and there are many examples where the same species has been allocated different names. The most recent revisions of genus fuchsia have now helped clarify the issue.

What is confusing to many is the use of a Latin name. When this was first introduced, all the hybrids and variants were given Latin names, usually by the raiser or introducers. Sometimes the raiser named them after themselves e.g. F. dominiana, F. thompsonii, or they described the flowers e.g. F. globosa, F. longipedunculata, F. conspicua. This was all very confusing in that the use of **a Latin name** does not indicate that the plant is a species. This practice is now no longer allowed.

Another problem which has arisen in recent years, is the naming of plants which have been grown from seed of a species. Some of these have slight differences such as dwarf habit, darker coloured leaves, more free flowering etc. and have been given cultivar names. Examples are Shuna Lindsey and Lechlade Goblin, both of which originated from seed of *F. denticulata.* Whereas there is no rule which specifically rules out the practice, it would be far better, if and when such plants are introduced, that they are given a varietal name e.g. *F. denticulata* var. Lechlade Goblin.

VARIETAL NAMES. Plants arise, usually from seed, which may have originated in the wild, which are undoubtedly the same species, but have slight botanical differences. Some of these have been cultivated for many years and to identify them, horticulturists who desire to know exactly what is being cultivated have given them varietal names.

Examples of these are :-

F. fulgens gesneriana, F. fulgens rubra grandifolia, F. fulgens goselli
F. boliviana alba, F. magellanica gracilis, F. magellanica alba.

CULTIVATION. A few species have been cultivated in Europe for many years, and are not difficult to grow. The most common being:-

F. fulgens and variants These plants are tuberous rooted and will often be late in the season before they show any signs of growth. However they grow very rapidly and soon come into flower. Any good compost will suffice, the plants perform better if grown outdoors in summer. Once the plants start to flower they will flower continuously until late Autumn, when they should be allowed to become dormant and wintered in a frost free environment. Repotting is best done in Spring when the first signs of growth appear. They do make a large plant given the right conditions.

F. boliviana and F. boliviana Alba. Very similar to the above, except they have a fibrous root system, and come into growth early in the season. Again they make a large plant, and are best grown outdoors during the Summer. They require a frost free environment during the winter

F. arborescens and F. paniculata. These plants are very similar in that the flowers are born in panicles resembling a Lilac. F. arborescens has much the larger panicles, even so many times they are mistakenly misnamed. F. paniculata is an ideal plant for the show bench, being easy to cultivate and time for flowering. On the other hand F. arboreseens is difficult to shape and is irregular in flowering.

F. splendens. F. splendens and F. splendens/cordifolia come into flower very early in Spring and is a welcome sight when flowering profusely with red and green flowers in the greenhouse or conservatory. It will also put up a late flush of flowers during Autumn, but rarely flowers during the Summer.

F. denticulata. Although it can be manipulated to flower in mid to late Summer, its natural flowering time is early Autumn, and again with the right treatment will flower until very late in the year.

F. sanctae-rosae. A good natured plant which produces many orange flowers in Summer and flowering over a long period.

F. hartwegii. A plant that gives pleasure all Summer, with its bright orange flowers. It needs a strong prune during winter to prevent it becoming very straggly.

F. procumbens. A straggly trailing plant with heart shaped leaves, although hardy in most areas it is best grown in a hanging pot. Over feeding will result in foliage growth and few flowers.

Fuchsia species are a very interesting subject, with plants evolving in almost every climatic system, they require a very large learning curve to anyone who wants to study and cultivate them. With many, just trial and error will lead to successful cultivation. Most of what is available commercially will be easy to grow and give immense pleasure.

ENCLIANDRA FUCHSIAS

By T. Strickland

It is encouraging to see many more of this type of fuchsia being exhibited, being one of the most popular classes at the shows in recent years. Identified by their small flowers, usually less than half an inch long and small leaves. This section has been called **'Breviflorae'** (Short flowered).

There are six species..-

F. microphylia with six sub species

microphylia, hidalgensis, quercentorum, aprica, hemsleyana and chiapensis.

F. encliandra with three sub species

encliandra, tetradactyla and microphylloides.

F. thymifolia with two sub species

thymifolia and minimiflora.

F. obconica

F. cylindracea

previously parviflora.

F.ravenii

The hybrid

Fuchsia microphylia x thymifolia is called **x bacillaris.**

Names which are old or incorrect:-

F. notarisii, F. mixta, F. minutiflora, F. uniflora, F. minutiflora var hidalgensis, F. michoacanensis, F. striolata, F. chiapensis, F. heterotricha, F. bacillaris, F. hemsleyana, F. pulchella, F. pringlei, F. colimae, F. minimiflora, F. biflora, F. tacanensis, F. skutchiana, F. parviflora, F. acynifolia, F. tetradactyla,

F. seleriana, F. striolata, F. mexiae.
Encliandra's originate from the mountains of Mexico growing high in the tropical rain forest some 10,000 feet or more. The name is Greek and it means 'Enclosed Male', because only four stamens protrude beyond the rim of the tube instead of the usual eight. A number of crossings have been made in recent years between Encliandras and paniculate flowered fuchsias, but some of these have paniculate type flowers, for example Edith Hall. These should not be shown in encliandra classes at shows.

Cultivation of encliandras present little difficulty but they should not be overpotted, they like a soil based compost. Ideally suited for small pot culture and bonsai. Some also can be grown into medium sized structures.

Pale colours are best grown in semi-shade, reds will take full sun but all dislike high temperatures. Given enough light and kept frost free, encliandras will flower all the year round, so you should never be without flowers in the greenhouse.

Within the encliandra range of fuchsias, we have six that are scented, (two species and four cultivars), these are..-
F. thymifolia (ssp minimiflora).
F. thymifolia (ssp thymifolia).
James Travis.
Jimmy Cricket.
Little Catbells.
Neopolitan.

Hopefully more scented ones will be released over the coming years. Most encliandra fuchsias you see today are forms of Fuchsia x bacillaris and are named, approximately 100 in total.

Recommended for you to try, are any of the following;-

Fiona Pitt,	Neopolitan,	Fuksie Foetsie,	Lottie Hobby,
Radings Karin	Chapel Rossan,	Karen Isles,	Katinka,
Obcylin	Snowflake,	Syijon,	T.S.J.

GROWING BONSAI FUCHSIAS

By R. G. Payne

Selecting and growing of a Bonsai Fuchsia.

In growing Bonsai fuchsias , the aim is to create a flowering tree in a small pot . Always keep this in mind when selecting a fuchsia to create a bonsai subject [see list]. The encliandra species or the encliandra cultivars, have a small leaf and flower which makes them an excellent initial choice. Having selected your plant it should be grown using the following techniques. Place potential Bonsai plants in half pots starting with a 2.5cm (1") then 7.5cm (3") half pots continuing in increments of 2.5cm (1") upwards 20cm (8"), or a half or full seed tray , these are then used for shaping etc til it is ready for its final dish..

During this growing period inspect closely from all angles, nominating 'the viewing position' or 'the front ' (appendix 1-3) always keeping in mind that you need to create a tapered trunk (fig 1).

This applies to all styles see groups 1 to 3. If the trunk is of an even thickness you can achieve a tapered trunk by cutting the leader just above a second or third axial, always at the back of tree so that the scar damage is not visible from 'the front' of the tree, appendix 2. The trunk can then be wired bending it into the required shape see (fig 2 to 4). This may need to be done several times, until you have achieved a natural tapering trunk, depending on the original size and style of the tree (fig 1). During this period the side branches are wired into position for forming initial pads, and left to grow and thicken. Once you have achieved your ideal trunk shape and thickness, you can start to form the leaf and flower pads . To do this, cut back to a pair of east - west leaf axil's on the branch chosen to be structured. Ultimate refinement are achieved by carefully cutting and wiring the side branches into an aesthetically pleasing structure, (figs 11-13). During this development, you will find that the natural tendency is for the branches at the crown of the tree to grow at a faster rate than the side branches. This needs attention in the early development of the tree by letting the bottom branches grow with only little pinching of the growing tips, whilst the branches at the top need shaping and wiring into place then pinching back hard until the bottom branches are fairly well developed. At this point you should have a tree worthy of a Bonsai dish.

It is best to take your tree with you to select a complimentary Bonsai dish, always ask the suppliers for their advice on the colour and shape of the dish.

PREPARING TREE FOR DISH.

This should be done in early Spring. Initially you need to cover all drainage holes with a fine mesh (fig 5) secured in place with wire clips (fig 6) [appendix] this helps prevent the compost being washed out and also helps to keep woodlice etc. out. (see figs 7).

You then thread a fine wire or string through the holes provided or drainage holes (fig 8) this will be used to secure the tree into place. Next place a fine layer of gravel over the base of your pot to assist with drainage, followed by a layer of fresh compost, (appendix). Now its time to prepare the tree roots for positioning in the Bonsai dish. Remove it from its growing pot in early Spring, just before any buds break. Gently tease out all of the roots, using a water spray to wash off all old compost. Cut and seal any tap roots, initially this allows you to see the amount of roots to be cut. They must all be cut and trimmed to about 2.5cm (1") of the inside of the dish, using knob cutters or sharp secateurs.(tools). After root trimming it is advantageous to soak the root ball in a solution of " Superthrive" (25 drops per gallon of water) for 10-15 mins. You now take the previously prepared dish, position the tree loosely on compost ensuring that it stands proud of the dish rim (fig 9), if this is not the case, add sufficient compost to do so, once its correct location is achieved, site the tree securely by gently pushing more compost between the roots using a chopstick, trying not to damage roots, remembering to place surface roots correctly. Take the securing wire and gently but firmly tie the tree into position.

Dressing of the tree.

Place some fine gravel on the surface and a light sprinkling of moss (appendix 7), once the pads start to break into growth you will need to cut and shape leaf and flower pads. Within 6-8 weeks the tree should be ready to enjoy and show (some species take longer, experience gained during previous growing periods will be a guide).

MAINTENANCE.

This total process will need to be repeated every 4 to 5 years. Annual maintenance will also need to be carried out as follows : -

(1) Root Pruning - to be done before new growth breaks, cut back 2.5cm - 9cm (1"- 3") from potedge, again treat rootball with "Superthrive", repot with new compost see (fig. 10).
(2) Branch pruning and shaping 4-6 weeks after root pruning and potting, trim and wire leaf pads-accordingly in order to maintain desired structure and shape.

TOOLS

1. Angle Cutters - are used to cut branches.
2. Knob Cutters - I use to cut roots and branches.
3. Bonsai Scissors - a good pair of Bonsai scissors or a sharp pair of scissors. Scaling Paste - this is used to seal any cuts you make on trunk you can take a piece of bark from a discarded branch and tape into place thus leaving no scar.
4. Secateurs - a good sharp pair is a must .
5. Fine copper coloured Aluminium (or bright aluminium wire but not on the show bench) wire, size to start with 1 mm, 2 mm, 3mm. You may need heavier gauge wire at a later date.
6. Rake - a large fork bent over to form a rake will suffice, you may have to remove some of the prongs, this is used to tease out roots.
7. Chopstick - this is used for pushing compost round roots.
8. Toothbrush or Fine copper brush - used for scrubbing trunk to remove moss and lime deposits.
9. Pair of tweezers - used for the removal of debris and any unwanted lichens also ideal to take out growing tips when trying to reduce leaf size.
10. Wire Snips - to cut wire from any trees after it has been used.
11. Pliers - to make wire clips used to secure drainage mesh

1. Appendix

1. The Viewing Position.
2. Use seal paste on all cuts to aid healing.
3. The Japanese always place their trees bowing towards them.
4. The Chinese viewing is all round.
5. Plastic Mesh - thick plastic greenhouse shading.
6. The B.F.S. have decided that Bonsai trees will be judged primarily viewing from the front position , but they will always take into account the overall picture you have created , healthy plant free of pests etc as per judges schedule.
7. Moss - collect a small quantity in a clean dry paper bag and place in the top of the airing cupboard to dry, then crush to a fine dust to sprinkle over your

bonsai tree dish surfaces this is for decoration only do not let it run riot up trunk and over hanging dish etc.

2. COMPOSTS

A free draining compost is a must with Bonsai I have used various types of mixes but have found that its best to experiment to what suits your growing methods.

Mix. 1. 2 Parts gravel, 1 Part composted bark [riddled]. 2 parts John Innes No 3, 2 Parts Multi Purpose compost.

Mix. 2. 2 Parts Gravel, 1 Part Perlite, 3 Parts John Innes No.3, 3 Parts Multi Purpose compost

Mix. 3. 3 Parts Gravel, 1 Part River Sand, 4 Parts Composted bark [riddled], 4 Parts Multi Purpose Compost. Or try one of your own, it must be free draining

3.Fuchsia List.

Ariel, Cottingham, Devon Cornish Pixie Bell, Derby Imp, Fuksie Foetsie, F. *encliandra*-encliandra, F. *magellanica,* F. *pumila,* F. *microphylla,* F. *versicolour,* Junes Butterfly, Lottie Hobby, Logan Gardens, Tea Room, Oosje, Oulton Fairy, Oulton Bonsai, Radings Inge, Radings Karin.

Just a few of many to choose from, these have made or will make an excellent Bonsai to be enjoyed by you and all that view them when on display.

Fig.1 Fig.2 Fig.3

Fig. 4

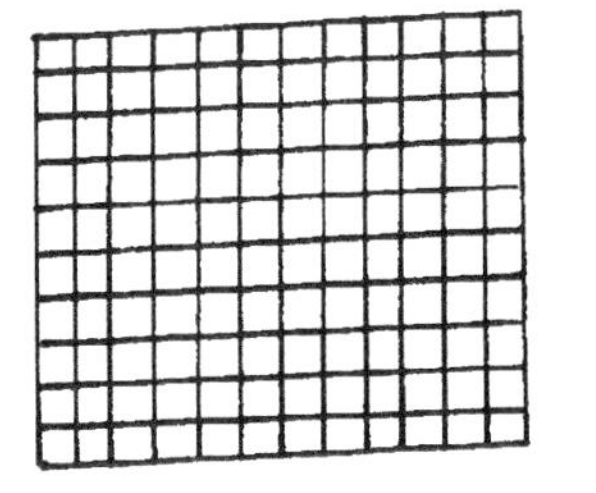

Fig. 5 Mesh

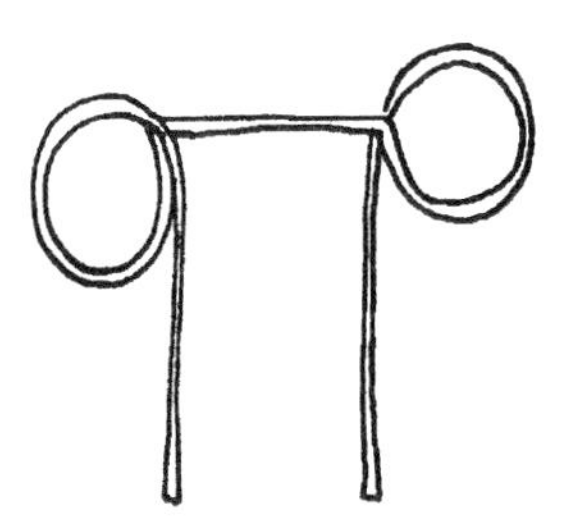

Fig. 6 Wire clip

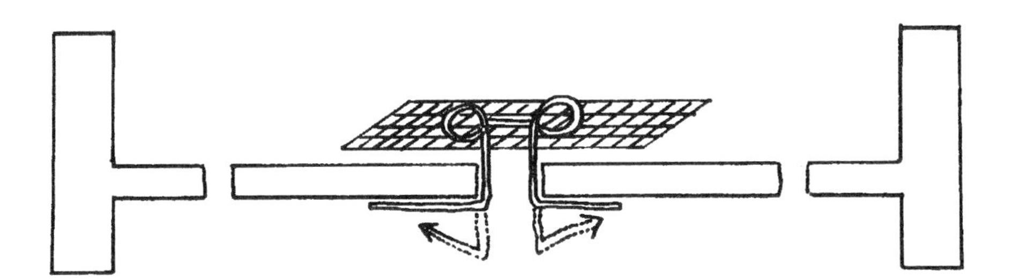

Fig. 7

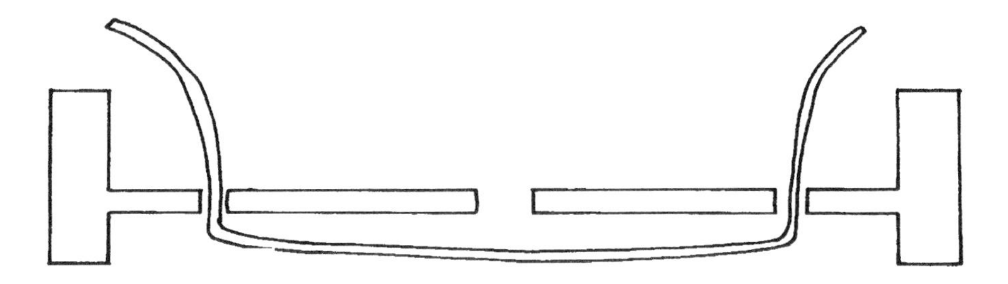

Fig. 8 (wire or string)

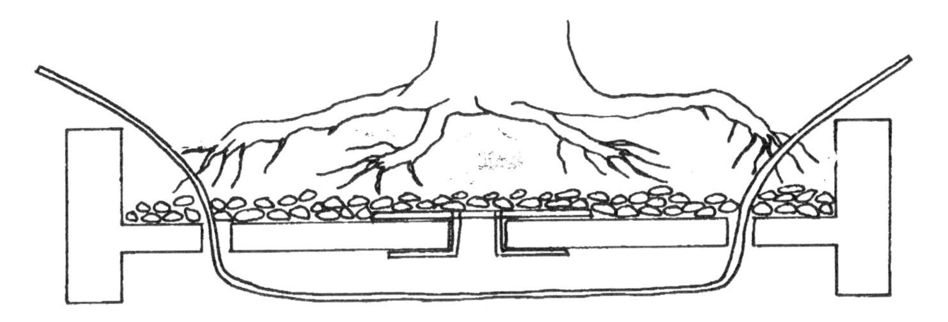

Fig. 9 (Bare root)

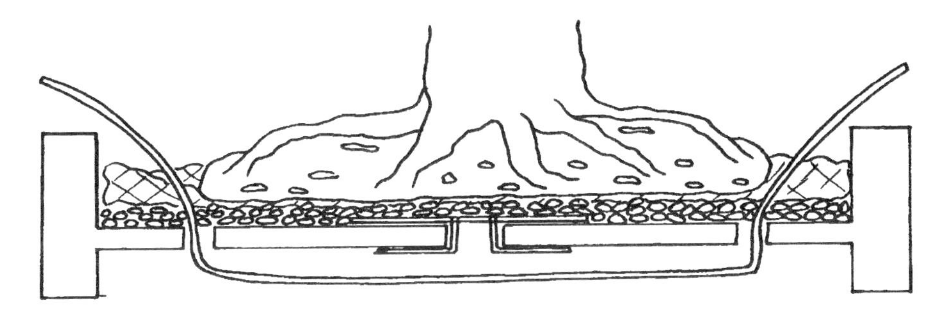

Fig.10

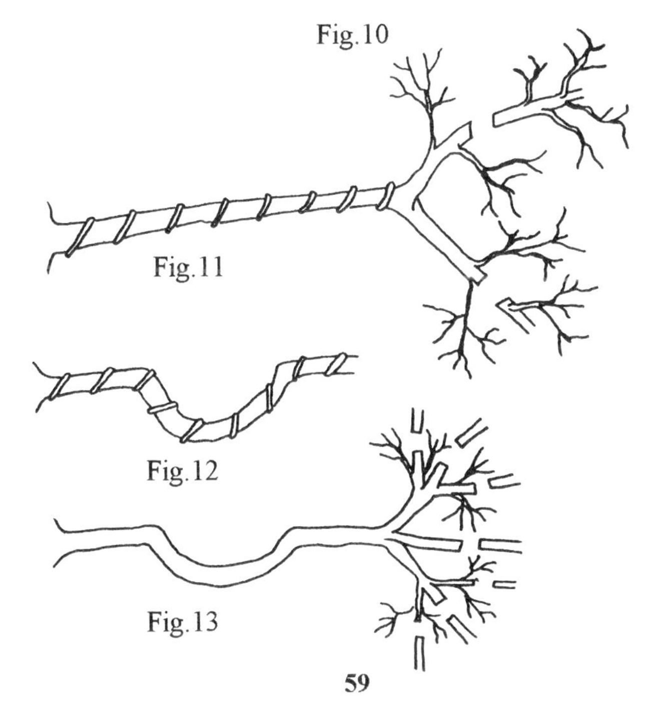

Fig.11

Fig.12

Fig.13

STYLES OF BONSAI

CASCADE. "kengai" plunging downwards , full cascades are usually in a tall square,or round pot to balance weight of cascade.
SEMI -CASCADE. "han-kengai" is not a full cascade and ends just above feet of pot.
FOREST STYLE. "yose - us" number of trees used some times starts about 11 but numbers do not matter, but the overall picture is most important.
GROUP PLANTING. "sambon - yose" the arrangement is in odd numbers 3.. better arrangements are derived from odd numbers. 5 "gobon-yose" and so on .
LANDSCAPE PLANTING. "bonkei" this is a rock, planted with cultivars to form a landscape, sometimes other types of plants are used to give the impression of bushes and flowers growing.
RAFT STYLE. "bunjingi" this is a fallen tree where the branches have rooted to grow and form trees.
CLUMP STYLE. “kabudachi" this is where a tree has been felled, and new trunks have grown from it, very rare and hard to produce, akin to pollarding .
DRIFTWOOD STYLE. "shriniiki" this is where a piece of driftwood has been used for visual impact where one or more trees have been bonded onto the driftwood, then grown on to form a very dramatic style.
BROOM STYLE. "bokidachi" this is probably the most tree like of all bonsai styles and consists of a number of branches all issuing from the same point at the top of an upright trunk, these branches divide and sub divide regularly until they form a fine tracery of twigs.
FORMAL UPRIGHT. “chokkan” the ideal "chokkan" bonsai will have a straight trunk with uniform taper and branch structure and an overall conical shape, the roots should spread out in a uniform base.
LITERATI. "bunjigi" the style is a chinese name meaning, men of books, the tree rises obliquely with a trunk that is bare of branches, except at the TOP.
ROOTS over ROCKS. "sekijoju" this is where the roots are placed to give a dramatic effect of a tree growing on the top of a rock and the roots have climbed over and into the rock and down into the earth.
SINUOUS STYLE. "netsurangari" this is where several trees all grow from the same root, the trees themselves may be individually trained in any style which suits the cultivar used, natural netsurangari are root suckers.
TWISTED TRUNK STYLE. "nejikan" a number of whips are plaited together to form a trunk, over the years they will form a solid trunk when shaped and styled.

TWIN TRUNK STYLE. "sokan" this is where you have more than one trunk growing from the base of a single trunk, all trunks must be at soil level not just above. This includes kabudachi style where you have multiple trunks growing from a single root .
WINDSWEPT STYLE. "fukinagshi" this style represents a tree growing on exposed sea cliffs and mountain tops swept by winds and storms.
EXPOSED ROOT STYLE. "neagari" this is where the roots have been placed to give the impression of a tree on stilts .
SLANTING STYLE. "shakan" this is a most satisfying style to accomplish, the name implies instability, there is no doubt that aesthetically to balance an inclining form which defies gravity is no easy task, to compensate for this you need to provide a visual counterbalance, this is achieved by building a supporting buttress of roots or compost to imply an equal and opposite force or by placing a branch on the opposite side of incline.

FUCHSIAS IN THE GARDEN

By D. Luther

Many of us plant hardy and non hardy fuchsias directly into the ground and then worry, should we dig them up or let them take their chances through the winter. Those chosen to be planted directly into the ground need to have been grown in at least 11.25cm (4½") pot and planted out at the end of May or beginning of June depending on which part of the country you live. The dilemma is what to do when winter approaches. You have to make the decision at planting time and I have two different methods. If I decide that some varieties might have a chance of surviving through the winter along with recognised hardies I plant in the following manner.

Dig a hole 7.5cm (3") or 10cm (4") deep 30cm (12") to 37.5cm (15") across, now at this new soil level make a suitable size hole to accommodate the root ball. I like to mix one part peat to two parts of the soil that has been excavated, add to this some blood, fish and bone fertiliser and mix well. Offer the plant to the hole and if satisfied that the best aspect of the plant is facing the way that you want it, plant firmly and water in. Do not fill in the 7.5cm (3") 10cm (4") x 30cm 1(2") 37.5cm (15") hole. Leave the remaining soil around the circumference of the hole and as you water, weed, hoe etc., this soil will gradually work back in and give the crown of the plant an extra three to four inches of protection. If all the soil were replaced at the start, soil borne bacteria could attack the soft growth and kill the whole plant. Do not forget to look after the watering needs of these plants until well established. Often it is suggested that you place three plants of the same variety in a group, when I do this I plant them as close together as possible, so that if one should die the remaining will grow into the space.

If you want your plants to have a better chance of survival they have to be dug up and given frost free protection. Follow the previous planting instructions but ignoring the deeper planting advice. When winter approaches the cold weather generally catches us out, and we have to dig them up in a hurry, and it was due to these circumstances that I adopted the following procedure. You will need carrier bags or similar, twine and labels. The plants I have to deal with are 1.8m (6') to 2.4m (8') tall but the following could apply to any type of growth. Dig up each plant in turn trying to keep the root ball intact, but if you do not manage it, do not worry. Place roots into one of the bags, small root ball small bag, making sure that sufficient soil is included to prevent roots drying out. Use a piece of twine to tie the bag firmly around the stem attaching a label indicating variety, or at least sufficient information so that the plant can be identified in the Spring. To prevent pest and disease problems the soft growth and all the foliage have to be removed. Retie the plant to any supports so that there will be no problem when moving them. The plants I deal with being so tall have to be laid flat in a cellar, so after laying them down I make a small hole on the upper side of the bag to facilitate watering if required. To keep them frost free they can he covered with any insulating material, moss peat is ideal as it can be used as a mulch after planting out. Check occasionally to ensure that the plants are not drying out. It is important to keep the root ball moist on all tall fuchsias so as the stems do not dehydrate. This is what causes most to die back and just leave you with a bush in the spring instead of what you expect to be a lovely standard, pillar or other large structure. The cellar could be a garage, shed, greenhouse or if you have a well drained garden, a hole in the ground. If you decide to bury your plants in the garden they are quite safe as long as the topmost part of the plant is covered by at least nine inches of soil. Mark this site with pegs.

The plants are left in their winter quarters until you judge that it is safe to bring them out. On removing them from their hibernation gently tease out old soil trying not to damage the new roots, old roots can be pruned and using good quality fresh compost pot the plants into the smallest pot that will comfortably take the roots. Water to help consolidate the compost. The plants may have young white shoots (etiolated) which are removed and is soon replaced with fresh growth. Because I live on the south coast I put the plants outside after the 14th April as on average this is the date of the last frost. I place the pots against a north facing wall so that they do not have to endure the heat of the sun, therefore responding better to a more average day to night temperature. If there is an unexpected late frost protect with some type of material, fleece is excellent for this job. I have been told by an expert in the field of pests and diseases, that if you wrap the root ball of your standards or other specimen fuchsias in Fleece 25, tying the fleece around the stem and placing plant back into the container, dressing the top with compost, this will prevent vine weevils from laying their eggs and the grubs from entering the root ball.

When fuchsias are planted out permanently, care must be taken when hoeing as some varieties are shallow rooted. You may have noticed that the roots run three or four inches below soil level for two or three feet before sending out feeder roots. In my experience I believe it is important to protect these roots from the sun. I looked after a bed of fuchsias that was in full sun, and the only shade was that provided by themselves. Annually they were given a mulch of good garden compost and a dressing of Vitax Q4. This was supplemented with an occasional few handfuls of Growmore during the season.

So that the fuchsia bed is not bare during the winter and spring, inter plant with bulbs, as they do not interfere with fuchsias, and their foliage gives added protection. Snowdrops, scillas, dwarf daffodils are good and crocus can been planted round the edge of the bed. The choice of fuchsia is yours, do not be frightened to experiment with different varieties, but any from the B.F.S. hardy list will do fine. Check on heights before you plant.

Do not prune these fuchsias until the Spring when new shoots are seen as the branches and twigs help to protect the crown of the plant, but if the plant is interfering with others or obstructing the pathway prune back the minimum amount required. In the Spring the amount you remove is dependent on how large you require the plant to be. To list fuchsias suitable to be planted out permanently is an impossible task as those that are suitable are totally dependent on the area you live and other factors concerning your garden. Would you be able to grow these as hardy in your area? Swingtime, Gay Fandango, Orange Mirage, Thalia, Annabel, Prosperity, Barbara, *F. fulgens* (does not flower though). My advice is to look round the neighbouring gardens in your area and see what does well and try one or two that you think might succeed.

PATIO POTS, TUBS AND WINDOW BOXES.

Most fuchsias will grow happily in any type of container as long as it has sufficient drainage holes, but make sure that the chosen container is thick enough to prevent the heat of the sun scorching the feeder roots. Fuchsias do well grown on their own but can be a good addition to a mixed container. Thought must be given to the suitability of fuchsias for this purpose, habit of growth e.g., upright or trailing, colour and size of flowers, size of leaves and would it be too vigorous for the companion plants? Try and plan the colour combination of all the types of plants being used. Strong bold, even clashing colours can be used to good effect, but beware of falling into the trap of just using deep blue lobelia with red and white fuchsias and inadvertently becoming patriotic. The following **trailing** plants seem to do well when grown together and with fuchsias: Petunia Surfinia, Verbena, Lobelia*, Begonia*, Ivy Leaved Geraniums and Sutera. Additional **foliage** plants can be added: Chlorophytum elatum variegatum, Helichrysum, Lysimachia, Plectranthus and Nepeta hederifolia variegata and not forgetting the many variegated fuchsias. There are also suitable **upright** versions of some of the plants: Petunia*, Geranium, Verbena, Lobelia* plus Busy Lizzie*, Ageratum*, French Marigold*, Tagetes*, and many other summer bedding plants that can be used. The inclusion of scented plants can give an extra dimension: Allyssum*, Petunia and Nemesia are three suitable for this purpose. Fuchsias, Petunia Surfinia, Verbena, Sutera, Nemesia, Ivy Leaf Geraniums,Geraniums and the foliage plants all benefit from being pinched out.

Remove the Spring flowering plants from your containers and dispose of all the old compost and replace with a good quality potting compost. The old compost can be used as a mulch or put onto your compost heap. It is far better to have one good container of plants rather than several mediocre examples. Remove the pots from the expensive plants that you have chosen . Put sufficient compost into the container so that when you place the pots inside the container they are at the correct depth, making sure that each pot is in the correct position for the plant it contained. Fill the gaps and pots with compost. Now put in all the cheap plants like lobelia allyssum etc., and when this task is completed carefully remove the pots one by one replacing each with it's corresponding plant. This way you will avoid breaking pieces from your more expensive plants. Water sufficiently to settle the compost and if possible stand your containers in a semi- shaded area for a few days so that the plants can get acclimatised to their new conditions. It is better to give them a good watering and let them nearly dry out before watering again. A splash and a dash is not the answer. More plants die through over watering than probably any other reason. If your life style prevents you from being able to keep a close eye on their watering needs you should consider adding a water retaining gel to the compost.

Try to inspect your containers at least twice a week and give them a quarter turn if possible. Inspect them for pests and diseases. Remove any dead or dying leaves and flowers. Remove seed pods as this will prolong the flowering period of most plants that you are likely to use. There should be no need for supplementary feeding for at least six weeks after planting. If needed, any high potash fertiliser will do. If you are not sure what to buy, any fertiliser recommended for tomatoes would be fine.

At the end of the season many of the plants can be over wintered, the ones listed* are generally grown from seed but the rest with the exception of geraniums and chlorophytum elatum variegatum are repotted and cut back within 5cm (2”) of the compost, this will encourage plenty of new growth, and during January - March cuttings can be taken. Geranium cuttings are taken in August and chlorophytums are grown from their little plantlets. In the spring the mother chlorophytum can be cut back to compost level and you will be well rewarded with nice new growth.

When choosing plants for a container I try to visualise the final effect so that there is harmony of colour, leaf size and texture. If possible at least one scented plant. Now think about the following combination of plants. Fuchsia 'La Campanelia' semi double trailer. Fuchsia 'Parkstone Centenary' double upright. Fuchsia 'Preston Guild' single small flowered upright, all of these are white and purple. Fuchsia 'Panylla Prince' pink/mauve encliandra type flower. Sutera 'Sea Mist' white. Sutera 'Knysna Hills' mauve. Nemesia 'Confetti' mauve and scented. Verbena 'Pearl' pearl coloured. Verbena 'Temari' white. Petunia small flowered mauve. Lobelia white and rose types. Helichrysum compact silver or Fuchsia 'Tom West' to be grown for the foliage only, so remove the flowers. These have a common colour theme and each type of plant compliments another and carries the texture of one variety into another. Look at other peoples efforts, note the ones you like and pinch their ideas. If you are going for a red or yellow theme think about using Nasturtiums, all you need to do is put some seed around the edge.

Whatever you decide to grow the most important thing is to dispose of all the old compost, and use good quality fresh potting compost. If you only need a small amount buy a good quality Growbag and use it's contents. You can even use the Growbag as the container.

What ever! Have fun.

OVERWINTERING.

By P. Boor

The fuchsia is a deciduous plant that will normally drop its leaves in the Autumn and go naturally dormant in winter.
Not all the species and cultivars require the same conditions to ensure their survival in our winters. Generally their requirements may be divided into three separate groups listed below:-

- **a)** Those that are regarded as hardy and may be permanently planted in the open ground.
- **b)** Those plants in pots, containers and baskets including those recognised as hardy.
- **c)** Those of the Triphylla type, any very young plants and those being grown on the biennial method.

Now we will consider the requirements of each group.

Group a:- Very little need be done to ensure that this group will survive. The plants may be tidied up by cutting back any straggly growths, lay a little straw or hay over the crown of the plant and rake up about 15cm (6") of soil over the straw or hay. This should be sufficient to ensure their survival. Do not cut the plants too severely as the stems will provide some protection for the crown. However new growth will usually start from the crown in spring at which point the old dead wood can be removed to where the new growth appears.

Group b:- This group will require to he kept frost-free during winter. Prepare your plants at the end of September or early October by cutting back by about one third and cutting off the remaining leaves. Spray using a combined insecticide/fungicide mix, together with the cutting off of the leaves this should ensure that you do not over winter pests and diseases. Now the plants are prepared we must consider where to keep the plants in the frost-free conditions they require. The majority of us should be able to provide one of the following methods:-

1. Burying in a trench in the Garden. Dig a trench at least two feet deep and large enough to contain all your plants, line the bottom of the trench with straw or hay and lay the plants on their side, cover with straw or hay and replace the soil which should be at least six inches deep. Do not forget to mark the extent of the trench. In late spring uncover the trench and remove the plants. You should see lots of long white growths, these can be cut back, and your plants will soon revert to normal green growth.

2. In boxes in a frost- free area. Line a box with polystyrene tiles or old packing, lay the plants on their sides and fill between with moist peat. The boxes can he kept in any frost free area such as a shed, garage or any unheated room in the house. The plants will require looking at every three weeks and watered sparingly if required.

3. Unheated greenhouse. Lay the plants on their side under the staging, cover with moist peat making sure that the plants have at least six inches cover. In very severe weather an old blanket or sacking will give added protection. It is possible to leave your plants on the staging and cover them with newspaper and/or horticultural fleece but they will require extra protection during particularly cold spells. Once again do not forget to pay attention to occasional watering.

4. Cold Frame. Line the frame with polystyrene or old carpet, put three inches of peat on the bottom and lay your plants on their sides and cover with moist peat. The frame may be covered with old blankets, carpet or sacking if the weather is particularly cold. Again do not forget the watering. Lining the greenhouse with polythene or bubble film will provide a few extra degrees of protection, bubble film is the best option. Prior to returning your plants to the greenhouse it is essential that the house is thoroughly cleaned and disinfected.

5.Heated Greenhouse. With the exception of any very young plants and those growing on the biennial method you only require a temperature of between 1-3°C (34-38°F) to keep your plants just ticking over but not actively growing. Regular checks for water are a must. I would suggest at least weekly.

Group c:- For those plants growing on the biennial method and any young plants or cuttings a temperature of 5-7°C (40-45°F) will need to be maintained. A weak feed of balanced food should be given at least once a month. Regular turning of the plants and attention to any pest or disease is vital to their health at this time as of course is watering. Keep the plants just moist. When possible do open the vents and doors when weather permits. Try and complete any watering as early as possible in the day. A layer of fleece over the plants will provide added protection in the event of severe frosts. Before returning any plants to the greenhouse make sure that the house is thoroughly cleaned and disinfected. Lining the house with bubble film will also save on heating costs.

To restart any dormant plants into growth in the spring simply spray the plant with tepid water in the morning and evening. You should soon see new growth at this time, remove the plant from its pot and take away as much of the old compost as is possible. Repot into a size smaller pot using fresh compost and when the plant is growing away strongly you can then prune if necessary.

With a little care and attention most of your plants should survive to grow on and give you pleasure for a further year. Remember to keep them frost free and watered regularly and you should not have too many losses.

GROWING FUCHSIAS WITHOUT A GREENHOUSE.

By B. Price Trasler.

The growing of Fuchsias without a greenhouse requires more patience than usual but the end results are very rewarding with lovely plants for the garden and show bench.

HOW do you get started ? From January onwards it is possible to buy plants from specalist fuchsia nurseries and some garden centres. If you are new to fuchsia growing I would not buy rooted cuttings, go for plants in 6.25cm (2.5") pots. If you don't know a specalist nursery in your area look out for adverts in the gardening press where there are usually many adverts in the spring.Failing that contact your local fuchsia society for help, most are listed at your local central library or contact the British Fuchsia Society for help. This address is listed else where in this book but don't forget to enclose a stamped, addressed envelope.

WHAT should you look for when buying a plant? Look for a plant that looks nice and healthy but not necessarily the biggest plant on sale. Make sure the leaves are even sized (dia 1) and make sure that in each leaf joint there is a shoot (dia 2). Even sized leaves should mean a good root formation,missing shoots at the leaf joints will mean missing side branches and an uneven plant. It will be highly unlikely that the shoots will develop at a later stage.

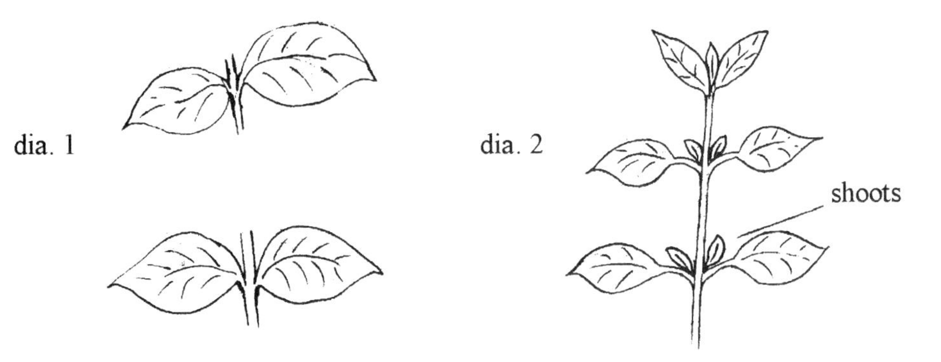

NEVER buy too many plants - most fuchsia growers do so and then there is disappointment because they can't be looked after properly. You are new to fuchsia growing so stick, say, to six bush plants in your first year and look for single or semi-double flowered varieties. this way you will get lots of flowers on your plants.You may like the big double flowered varieties but you will not get many flowers during the season.A specalist fuchsia nursery will advise you on the best and easiest single/ semi-double varieties to grow.

SINGLE/semi double flowers, what does this mean? All fuchsia flowers have four sepals which are the petals which stick out at the bottom of the tube but the skirt below the sepals (correct name is corolla) only has four petals in single flowered varieties and in semi double flowers there are between five and seven petals. Double flowers have eight or more petals.

WHAT preparations should I make before I bring my plants home? Choose where you are going to grow your plants the ideal situation is a windowledge that faces either north or east. A south or west facing situation could get a lot of sun, even in the winter and your plants would need shading so that they did not get too hot. Thought must also be given to night protection as to leave your plants on a cold windowledge with the curtains drawn behind them is asking for trouble. The wisest thing to do is to lift your plants into the room for the night or place polystyrene tiles between the plants and the glass. If the weather gets very cold the tiles will not give enough protection and plants must be moved. Think of your plants as little babies.

A LIGHT box constructed from a cardboard box and lined with cooking foil is a good way to make sure your plants get as much light as possible in the dark days at the start of the year (dia 3). When the light rays fall on the foil in the box they are reflected back on to your plants. Plants will need turning every three days - just a quarter turn, use your plant label as a guide and decide if you are going to turn your plants to the left or right each time you turn them.When you have decided if you are a left turner or a right turner stick to the same direction all the time. AND mentioning labels, NEVER take them out of the pot - why? will you remember which label goes where? You may wonder why you are being told to turn your plant - because otherwise they will be drawn towards the light and the plant will grow lanky and lopsided.

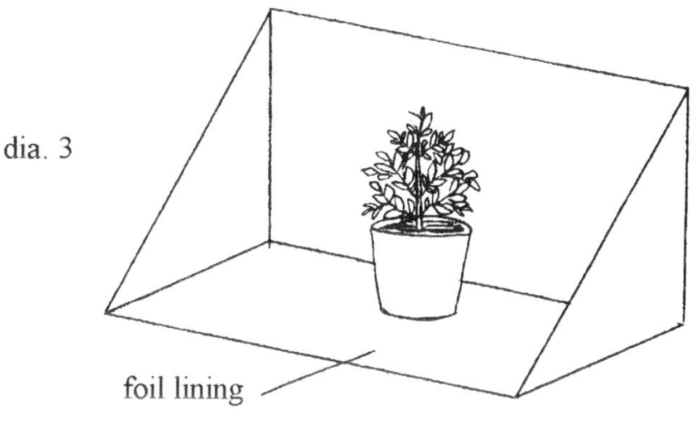

WATERING plants has to be done with care especially in winter. It is important not to let your plants get too dry as it will kill them and the same thing will happen if you over water them. Learn to gauge the water in the compost by the weight of the pot. When you get home with your plants hold a pot in your hands and try to remember how heavy it feels, a few days later do the same again and you will find it feels lighter - if it feels very much lighter water the plant well and let all the surplus water drain away, you will now find that the pot feels really heavy. Your plant will not need water again until it feels as light as it did before you watered it. In the wintertime this could be two to three weeks. With practice you will be able to judge when your plants need watering.

AFTER a few weeks look at the bottom of your pots and you may well see little roots coming out through the holes this could mean that your plants are ready for potting on into a bigger pot. If you place your fingers over the top of the pot, without damaging your plant, turn it upside down again and give the edge of the pot a sharp tap and you will be able to lift the pot off the root ball and have a look, if the roots are running around the bottom now is time for a larger pot. The compost you use is your choice, some growers make up their own composts and others use growbag compost! There are many good composts available but I suggest that with only a few plants that you buy a small bag of your choice unless you have other plants you can use it up on. Fresh compost is always best. Just make sure that it is multi-purpose. Sieve the compost to make sure you do not have any lumps in it as they will make the job of potting on more difficult. Select a pot that is not more than 2.5cm (1") bigger than the one your plant is in now, place a little compost in the bottom of the CLEAN pot and gently place the root ball of the plant you are repotting in the new pot, make sure you place it centrally, and then trickle compost down the gap around the root ball. When the gap is filled give the pot a gentle tap - DO NOT FIRM THE COMPOST DOWN AROUND THE ROOTS - FUCHSIAS LIKE AN AIRY COMPOST.

ALL this time your plants have been growing and the little shoots in the leaf joints have become small branches with leaves on, when there are two pairs of leaves on these branches you need to remove the growing tip. Most new growers are horrified at the thought of doing this but it is necessary to get a nice bushy plant. When you have three pairs of branches growing you can nip out the main growing tip of the plant. When you get more profficient at growing fuchsias you will root this growing tip and have another plant. As each side shoot develops pinch their tips out after two pairs of leaves and you will have a nicely shaped plant growing on. You have to remember to keep turning the plants and potting them up into larger pots on a regular basis. There are chapters in this book which gives you a further explanation. You will also have to watch out for any pests which you can also read in another chapter as you can the feeding of your plants.

BY NOW your plants will hopefully, be getting nice and big and you will no longer be able to keep them on your windowledge. Most gardeners have a few polystyrene plant trays, find one who's indentations match the size of your pots this will be the resting place for your plants for the next few weeks. Fuchsias like fresh air and when it gets to mid April, providing it is not too wet or frosty you can put your plants outside in a sheltered, sunny position DURING THE DAY ONLY. They must come inside at night. As the days lengthen and get warmer you will be able to leave your plants out all the time BUT do listen to the weather forecasts and be prepared to put your plants under cover if frost is forecast - remember - in parts of the UK there can be frosts well into June.

WHEN do you stop stopping your plants? You could go on stopping indefinitely but you would not get any flowers! In your first year of growing stop pinching the tips out of the shoots at the beginning of May. You should then have flowers by July. The subject of timing your flowers is explained in another chapter. Towards the end of May you can start putting your plants in tubs etc., but do have frost protection at the ready-newspaper and fleece are both very good but not bubble plastic.

I do hope that you enjoy growing your plants so much so that you will invest in either a greenhouse or a deep coldframe to help with your new hobby - happy growing.

HYBRIDISING FUCHSIAS

By Gwen Rolt

Hybridising has been carried on for many years since the 19th century but where do those who wish to try for themselves find out how to go about the procedure. I acquired a book on Hybridising for Beginners and although it does not cover fuchsias the process is the same.

First of all what are you tying to achieve? Do you want to grow a plant that is like so many others already available or is it in order to give it a name? One has only to look at a large number of new introductions and wonder what it is that makes them different from many of the varieties already on the market. When registering a new variety one has to explain how your fuchsia is different or better than existing cultivars.

If you are really keen to hybridise choose a plant which you would like to use, in your project, one that has a good habit of growth and has plenty of flowers. You may decide to try to change the shape of the flower to one that is seen on another plant. Let us call the plant you wish to work with the 'mother' plant, this will be the one that has the pollen dusted over the stigma.

The blooms need to be almost ready to open, they can be 'popped' and pollen from another flower, the 'father' plant, can be passed over the stigma. You will know if the stigma is receptive as the pollen will adhere to it. The pollen, which comes on the ripening anther, can be transferred by removing the anther from the flower of the father plant and brushing it over the stigma of the mother plant.

Some hybridisers suggest using a camel hair brush for this purpose, the only problem with that is that the brush will need sterilising between each cross - a lengthy procedure. Once the cross has been completed protection of the stigma can be achieved by either covering the stigma with a small piece of protective material (fleece is ideal) or making up a small box frame covered in fleece and placing the whole plant in isolation. You can remove the anthers surrounding the stigma of the 'mother' plant to avoid self-pollination although other hybridisers I have spoken to feel that this is not really necessary as the conception has already taken place before the pollen is ripe.

It takes approximately seven weeks for the seedbearing berry to ripen; the berries can vary in colour from almost opaque through green, orange, red, and purple to black. When the berry is ripe it can be cut open with a sharp knife and the viable seed will show brown in colour and vary in size according to parent. The seed can be removed with the point of your knife and placed on a piece of kitchen paper, at this point I rub the seed across the paper to clean off any sticky substance, the seed can either be sown immediately or placed in a paper envelope to be sown at a later date. Seed needs light and warmth for germination and a little humidity helps as this stops the seed from drying out.

Specie seed will germinate even if it is not fully ripe whereas hybrid seed needs to be ripe. The life of the seed will deteriorate with the passing years, however I have had success with seed which is over three years old.

The most important work of the hybridiser is note taking; a record book is essential as the copious notes you will be recording will be useful with later crosses. When the cross has been carried out the easiest way of recording this is to write both parents on a label, the mother plant being the first name, electricians tape works well here, attaching that label to the stalk of the flower which is to be the mother, when the berry is removed the tape can be transferred, with the seed, to the label on the container in which the seed is to be sown. It is a good idea to note the date, time of day and the temperature at the time of the cross, for future reference. This can be used to advantage when working on further crosses. I have read that crosses should only take place when there is a thunderstorm about and preferably at mid-day, this would certainly curtail the number of crosses one could do in a year.

I have been practising the 'art' for several years and joined the Special Interest Group in order to further my knowledge. I was involved with work set up by the late Eric Johns when volunteers were given a plant of *F.lyciodes* and *F.magellenica* to try to raise the plant Rosea whilst I managed to get magellenica to accept pollen I did not manage to get lyciodes to do so.
This exercise got me more interested in the art of hybridising, what works and what doesn't.

Further experiments are going on with the SIG group, working with Paniculata and variegated Procumbens, again I have had some element of success with the former but the latter seems not to want to take the fertilisation to maturity.

I was given some good advice when I first embarked on this exercise, set yourself a task and follow it through something, which I now consider very carefully when

I am working with the plants.

My aim at the present time, is to try and get more hardy double flowered plants and to achieve this I have been using Tennessee Waltz with Empress of Prussia and with one of my own raising 'Baby Beverley', crossing both ways. I am sure some of these old cultivars have a lot to offer, after all they are still in most of the nurseries today.

You can of course, rely on the birds and bees to do the crossing for you and just take the ripened seed pods off the plants, be prepared for a large number of empty berries before you find seed, I do not get any satisfaction in doing this although I guess you could get a plant which is worth growing on.

Finally you must trial your new 'babies' for at least three years, showing them to professional growers to get their opinion, and have a large compost bin for the hundreds of seedlings which will not be worth pursuing.

If there are any other hybridisers who have useful information to impart I will be very pleased to hear from you; all information could be shared by other enthusiasts instead of it being lost.

WATERING AND FEEDING.

By J.V.Porter.

Watering and feeding is probably the most important aspect of growing fuchsias to a reasonable quality. Should either of these two important factors be missing or neglected then fuchsias will soon become either, weak spindly, sickly, yellow leafed, drop leaves and flower buds and be more attractive to pests, or even in some cases all of these problems.

Most potting composts that are manufactured come to us with a good fertiliser added. Which during the first few weeks will make a plant grow very quickly, but as the plant grows, it is also using up the goodness of the fertiliser all the time. Generally speaking after a period of approximately five weeks the fertiliser content of the potting compost will be almost, if not completely, exhausted of fertiliser. To ensure that the plant keeps healthy, it is therefore necessary to supplementary feed the plants. This can be achieved in several ways.

Perhaps the oldest method is to use organic fertilisers sprinkled on the surface of the pot every few weeks, the usual ones being dried blood, fish blood and bone or bone meal etc. Another quite acceptable practice would be to submerge a hessian sack of horse manure in a 200 litres (forty gallon) drum of water, leave for a couple of weeks until the water is the colour of weak tea, and it is then ready to water directly into the plant pots or containers.

The old ways proved very successful for grower's pre 1950, but with the growth of the farming and horticultural industries it became a necessity to use a more accurate method of feeding, and to develop a chemical fertiliser formulae to suit the different needs of every plant. Gradually with the help of this research, mixtures and ways of applying these fertilisers became available to the amateur grower.

To the beginner, a first time look into the field of fertilisers can be extremely confusing and/or off-putting. These are usually for mixing with water and although a powder, they are often referred to as *liquid fertilisers.* A study of the packaging reveals a list of the ingredients, a recommended amount to be added to water and the N.P.K. content of the feed.

Starting with N.P.K. It is known that N. (nitrogen) makes plants grow, which means an increase in size all round, however, too much N will give soft growth leaving it not strong enough to support itself, and even making the plant more susceptible to insect or fungal attacks. In shady conditions, feeding with to much N could be a total disaster by producing soft, spindly stems and over sized leaves. However, in sunny aspects N could be a great advantage, in making the plant grow during sunny weather conditions, which will normally ripen and harden plant growth, thus having a neutralising effect between bright sunlight and nitrogen feed.

P (phosphorus) is for root development and general health, phosphorus stays available to a plant for a longer period than other fertilisers and indeed some fertiliser compositions do not add any phosphorus at all. K (potash) ripens wood and sets/develops fruit and flowers, however too much of this element at the wrong time, i.e. sunny conditions, will give very brittle, stunted growth and small leaves and flowers. 1 have deliberately tried in this chapter to simplify the effects that the main fertilisers have on fuchsias, in reality it is not that simple but beginners, hopefully, will have been able to grasp the elementary aspect of feeding without difficulty. Therefore, and to sum up; it should be realised that N (nitrogen) and K (potash) have almost the opposite effect, as have bright light and shade therefore ***reduce N in shady*** conditions but increase K., and ***reduce K in bright*** conditions but increase N. Although understanding feeding can create problems at the beginning as soon as this understanding is grasped, better plants will be the result.

The application of liquid fertiliser will normally be recommended by the manufacturer to be applied every 7 to 10 days at a suggested rate. This will obviously be fine for fuchsias but many fuchsia growers adopt the method of mixing the fertiliser to a quarter of the suggested rate and use it every time they water their fuchsias, in other words a little at a time but more often.

Foliar feeding is another way of applying fertiliser to fuchsias. All fertilisers can be sprayed over fuchsias but may leave a residue on the leaves of the plants; to avoid this problem it is better to acquire a purpose made liquid fertiliser. It is best applied during bright weather conditions at a time when the leaves are aspirating. Many fuchsia growers do not bother with this form of feeding but it can be useful in giving a better leaf colour.

Liquefied seaweed organic products such as Maxicrop are not strictly fertilisers, but do act as stimulants. These can be applied at the recommended rate either as a spray or drench. An added usefulness of these products is the fact that it improves resistance to pests and disease.

PESTS and DISEASES

By J.V.Porter.

Fuchsias, when grown correctly, are certainly no more susceptible to attacks of pests or disease than any other plant. The key to a problem free crop of Fuchsias is, relentless attention to cleanliness, inspection and good husbandry of all plants in the collection. A fungus, of some description causes all diseases that occur on fuchsias.

Pests and disease are less likely to attack plants which are grown in clean, healthy surroundings and it is therefore of prime importance that, good hygiene is practised in the cultivation of Fuchsias. Debris such as fallen flowers and leaves should be cleared away daily, it is essential that special attention is given to the plants themselves, rotting flowers or leaves within the plant can quickly cause botrytis to spread into healthy tissue. Ventilation of a greenhouse environment is a must and will give a good flow of fresh air on which any fungi spores can float upwards and away through the vents. Any newly purchased or gifted plants should be kept away from the main collection for 14 days, to allow any pests or diseases to manifest itself in isolation, rather than risk the unwanted contamination of other plants.

During the autumn or winter months the greenhouse should be completely cleaned and sterilised to destroy any hidden insect eggs and fungi spores, once this has been done, ensure that any plants that are placed back inside are scrupulously clean, in some cases it may be possible to remove all the leaves from the plants, thus giving less places for eggs and spores to remain undetected.

Over recent years, many of the pests and diseases have built up immunity, to the pesticides and fungicides available to the amateur grower today, and it is therefore extremely difficult to eradicate any severe outbreak of pests or diseases. Constant vigilance on the part of the grower is therefore imperative, if early detection and action is to be achieved. It is wise to rotate spraying using three or four sprays of different base chemicals to avoid resistance.

Manufacturers of pesticides and fungicides always give full details of spraying and mixing instruction on the bottle or packet, which should always be adhered to. Details are also given with reference to the pests or diseases that the contents will control. Spraying is best done in the evening on a calm night with the vents closed, and if possible the air temperature of the greenhouse should be above 15°C (60°F). The following morning ventilate thoroughly to clear the greenhouse of fumes and excessive moisture.

APHIDS. Although there are many types of aphid, it is usually the greenfly that attacks the fuchsia. Eggs are normally laid on the underside of the leaves and in the tips of young shoots. After hatching the young greenfly nymphs suck the sap from the plant, causing distortion of the foliage. As greenfly grow to maturity, they shed their skins leaving the white membrane on the surface of the leaf below or dropping down to the compost, it is quite common for the cast skins to be mistaken for whitefly. The honeydew that greenfly produce attracts a black sooty mould, which although harmless to the plant is very unsightly and disfiguring, it is also an attraction to ants. Aphids in warm weather can swarm in great numbers, swarms can descend onto an area and infest plants instantly, they are known to travel across from France in summer. One of the favourite host plants of the greenfly is the Sycamore tree.

Control: Can easily be achieved by using one of the several brands of insecticide available, varying the chemical at each spray will help to avoid any pest resistance. A little washing up liquid in water will often give some control and also assist with the removal of sooty mould (the wise grower acts long before sooty mould is evident). The encouragement or introduction of natural predators, such as ladybirds, is highly desirable but insecticides cannot be used with this method of control.

CAPSID BUG, LEAF HOPPER, THRIPS: Are found mainly on fuchsias growing outdoors. They are small to minute insects that suck sap from fuchsias especially during early spring. They over winter in hedges of all description, hawthorn, privet, conifers or even in the base of fuchsias. Feeding on the tips of fuchsias their sucking action can cause damage, the worst of this being caused by the Capsid Bug, which injects a poison into the plant causing formidable distortion and blindness to the tips. Occasionally all three insects can cause problems in the greenhouse, especially thrip.

Control: Spray with a suitable systemic insecticide at 10 to 14 day intervals, starting as soon as fuchsia shoots are emerging in the spring, alternate the insecticide regularly, and continue until mid July. Capsids are usually less of a nuisance after this time, probably because the presence of flowers in the tips of the fuchsias is not as attractive as the succulent early season growth.

<u>FROGHOPPER:</u> (Cuckoo Spit). Froghoppers do not appear to do much harm, but the foamy froth it produces can be considered to be unsightly. The insect is very small and yellowish in colour.

<u>Control:</u> Wash away the froth with a spray of water, and spray with a suitable systemic insecticide.

<u>RED SPIDER MITE:</u> (Two spotted mite).
Red spider is very difficult to see with the naked eye, and its presence is very often undetected until irreversible damage has occurred. The key to successful combat with red spider is early recognition of the signs and symptoms of their occupancy of a plant.
Very slight silvery mottling on the upper surface of the leaves are the first signs of an infected plant. This often occurs firstly to the top leaves of the plant that is highest in the greenhouse; the reason for this is, that this will be the warmest and driest place, conditions in which the red spider thrives. The next stage is bronzing on the underside of the leaf, on which can be seen, with the help of a magnifying glass, adult red spiders. Excessive leaf fall will shortly follow, eventually leading to complete defoliation of the plant, it is only in extreme cases that a web will appear on a fuchsia plant but on fruit trees, a popular host plant for the red spider, web's are a regular occurrence. To avoid infestation by the red spider mite, a high humidity, cool temperature and good ventilation will discourage colonisation of the plants.

<u>Control:</u> Insecticides have limited effect, but suitable ones should be used alternately, to the manufacturer's instructions. There are biological controls available to the amateur grower, but these cannot be used in conjunction with insecticides. The foliar stimulant "Maxicrop" has been known to discourage the red spider from settling on fuchsia's when used at the recommended spray strength.

<u>SCIARID FLY</u>: A blackish grey fly about the size of a whitefly which lives on the surface of the compost within the plant pot or, can be found in great numbers wherever wet algae is present within the greenhouse. The adult fly causes no damage to fuchsias, it does however, bite some people and can be an annoyance, white threadlike larvae can sometimes be found in the potting medium, but they do little damage to the fuchsia.

<u>Control:</u> An aerosol household fly spray will easily eliminate the adult sciarid fly.

VINE WEEVIL: It is the maggot like larvae of the vine weevil, which cause the damage to fuchsias. Feeding on the roots of a plant they often remain undetected until the mutilation done causes the plant to topple over in its pot. On occasions the plant can be saved but it usually dies if not found early. Early indications of the presence of vine weevil are, smaller leaves on one plant when compared to the rest of the collection, looseness in the compost and neat semicircular bites out of the edges of leaves which indicates that the beetle like adults have been present and eggs have probably been laid in the compost.

Control: Is very difficult, Nematodes, a biological control can give some control over the grubs, with reports ranging from total success to total failure, it is obvious that the timing of the application and the temperature is of most importance. Always follow the manufacturers instructions diligently and ensure that the soil temperature does not fall below 10°C (50°F).
Compost is available to the amateur, which contains 'Intercept' a trade name for the chemical 'Imidacloprid', and has proved quite successful in eliminating the grubs. The same chemical is also available to mix, as a drench or spray but the cost in terms of money can be high.
Spraying thoroughly at dusk or a little later from March to July with a spray containing 'Bifenthrin or Pyrethrum' will help to keep down the adults and if a strict regime of spraying is carried out vine weevil can eventually be eliminated.

WESTERN FLOWER THRIP: A comparatively new pest to Europe the WFT (Western Flower Thrip) causes damage to, and shortens the life of fuchsia flowers, and is at its worst during warm weather. Bad infestations will cause some distortion to leaves. The very short, thread like insect, can easily be seen inside the flower but most difficult to find when amongst the foliage.

Control: Pick off all open flowers and spray with Malathion at regular intervals.

WHITEFLY: Perhaps the most troublesome pest of all. The small white, moth-like pest must never be allowed to breed unchecked in a greenhouse for more than three or four days, ignore this riule and whitefly will become almost impossible to eliminate.

Control: Constant vigilance is the answer; yellow sticky traps will first indicate the presence of whitefly in a greenhouse, look under the leaves of the fuchsias everyday and squash both adults and scales (eggs) with finger and thumb.

Insecticides have limited effect on whitefly and several sprays with different base chemicals, should be used alternately.
Biological control is available and may be of assistance, but remember, predators need whitefly as a food and will look elsewhere if they exhaust the source. Once the predator has left, back will come the whitefly.

There are several diseases that effect fuchsias, three of which attack the plant above soil level, i.e. Botrytis, Rust and Mildew. Below soil level there are many vague diseases which can cause damage, perhaps the most important being Pythium and Thielaviopsis often called sudden death syndrome.

BOTRYTIS: Botrytis or grey mould as it is sometimes calls is endemic in the atmosphere and starts off as a light brown rot, usually at the base of young cuttings, although, it can occur anywhere on a plant, on detached leaves and flowers, even on healthy flowers and stems higher up the plant. This fungi turns to a grey hairy form at a later stage in its developement, a sure indication that the spores will soon be airborne and will spread to new hosts. Contamination can also be spread by contact, with other plants or by utensils such as knives, scissors or even by human hands etc.

Control: Is by suitable fungicides such as Benomyl or Thiram, however, these have a limited effect and indeed can help to cause the wet conditions in which botrytis thrives, fresh air is a far better option. Even on the coldest of days it should be possible to ventilate for an hour or two and in milder periods ventilators should be opened as wide as possible for as long as possible. As long as freezing temperatures are not allowed, it is far better to ventilate for a few hours, than to keep a tightly closed atmosphere. A guide could be "if there is condensation on the underside of the glass ventilate" A recommended technique, if a severe outbreak occurs is to close the greenhouse, heat until the temperature reaches 27°C (80°F) and then open all ventilators and doors fully for 15 mins. Repeat this action all day and the botrytis problem will certainly reduce, if not completely disappear.

POWDERY MILDEW: A disease that has probably been with us for many years but was only identified in 1994. The symptoms usually occur in spring in the form of maroon/brown patches on the upper surface of the leaves, which at one time was thought to be caused by cold or sudden change, however upon close inspection a white powdery bloom can be seen, especially if the leaf is viewed obliquely to the light.

Control: In most cases the condition will clear itself after a month to six weeks. Spraying with tepid water early in the day will help to prevent or cure the problem, or a spray with "Nimrod T" should quickly clear the disease away.

RUST: Probably the most difficult to clear and the most problematic disease of them all. Rust has been with us for many years but has become more difficult over the last 20 years, perhaps strangely, this coincides with the reduction of coal fires and the resultant lower sulphur content of the atmosphere. The first signs of rust appear on the underside of the leaf as orange pustules (clusters of tiny dots), these eventually kill the tissue of the leaf and show through on the upper surface as dead, light brown patches. With good husbandry the problem will be spotted early and action taken immediately.

Control: Commercially, a fungicide called Plantvax 75 gives excellent results but amateurs have a little more difficulty. Tumbleblight and Systhane are too strong for fuchsias and, if used at full strength can distort the tips of the plants, however, diluted to half strength, little or no damage will occur, if used only occasionally. Therefore it should be possible to remove all infected leaves and burn or dustbin them before spraying to prevent a re-ocurrence of the problem. Spraying with a fungicide containing Thiram or Copper will give some protection as a preventative rather than a cure.

ROOT DISEASES: These are caused either by faulty or contaminated watering. Pythium for example is a pathogen, endemic in contaminated water supplies i.e. tanks, water butts etc. Problems will only be found in rooting cuttings, symptoms are; cuttings turning completely black and dying, often after rooting. Some control may be achieved by watering with a mild disinfectant before insertion of the cuttings, and disinfecting all benches, water containers and any utensil used in the production of cuttings.

Thielaviopsis (sudden death syndrome) will cause the collapse, suddenly, of a full grown plant, usually in hot weather. Stress is always an important factor in this problem, hot, dry conditions usually induce the grower to water when the temperature is above 27°C (80°F), or when a plant has wilted through a shortage of water, this causes the roots to expand too rapidly and burst, disease shortly follows and death shortly afterwards. Control of this problem lies with the grower, never water if the temperature is above 27°C (80°F), spray with cool water and remove to a cooler temperature, only water when the temperature has dropped to 18°C (65°F). Over feeding can also aggravate this problem.

OTHER PROBLEMS: Yellowing leaves, leaf drop and bud drop are caused not by a disease but by faulty watering or feeding. It is the growers problem to notice and recognise these symptoms of faulty husbandry and care, they may be caused by poor feeding or watering, dry atmospheric conditions, or simply by not knowing or understanding the conditions in which fuchsias will thrive and succeed.

Remember, if the growing conditions are correct, most of the diseases, with perhaps the exception of rust, are unlikely to cause problems.

CAUTION: Always store chemicals in a safe place away from children and follow the safety instructions. Be aware that they can harm humans and animals.

GLOSSARY

By C. Gubler

Biennial	Plants grown for two years before being allowed to flower.
Bonsai	A form of living art.
Bush	A fuchsia grown on a very short single stem 3.75cm (1.5").
Compost	A mixture of different ingredients specially prepared for taking cuttings or for growing on of plants.
Cultivar	Technical term for what is generally known as a variety.
Dormancy	A state of greatly reduced metabolism in which a plant is alive but not growing.
Double	Flowers which consist of more than eight petals.
Encliandras	Distinctive group of fuchsias, with small flowers (typically no larger than 1cm (0.4") in length) and foliage, with a shrubby type growth.
Feeding	The term used when additional nutrients are added to the water to supplement the nutrients already contained within the compost.
Foliage	The term given to the plants leafy growth can be either green or varigated (ornamental).
Hardy	The term used to describe varieties which are capable of surviving the winter planted outdoors in the garden.
Hybridization	The term used to describe the pollination of one plant with another to obtain new cultivars.
Leggy Plant	Term used to describe a plant that has produced long thin growth between internodes, usually caused from insufficient light.
Multi-plant	Where a number of plants or cuttings are grown together to look like one plant.

Over Potting	The term used to describe a plant that has been put into a pot which is too big for its size.
Petalloids	Extra but smaller petals.
Pruning	The term used to describe the cutting back of a plant to improve its shape or for winter.
Semi-double	Flowers which consist of five to seven petals.
Shrub	Fuchsia(s) grown with many stems coming from below the soil surface.
Single	Flower which consists of four petals.
Species	The "original" Fuchsias found in the wild in South America etc.
Sport	Sudden and permanent variation in flower or foliage.
Standard	A Fuchsia with a bushy head grown on a long stem.
Stopping	Removing the growing point to induce branching.
Sunscorch	Damage to leaf tissue caused by the plants being watered from above during strong sunshine.
Training	To tie in the shoots to obtain a desired shape.
Triphyllas	Distinctive group of fuchsias with characteristically long tube flowers, typically in clusters at the end of branches. Flowers are generally in the pinks, oranges and reds.
Virus	An agent, causing systemic disease, too small to be seen with the naked eye but very easily transmitted.
Whip	The term used to describe the running up of a single stem to produce a standard.
Woody	The term given to the ripening of the plant stems.

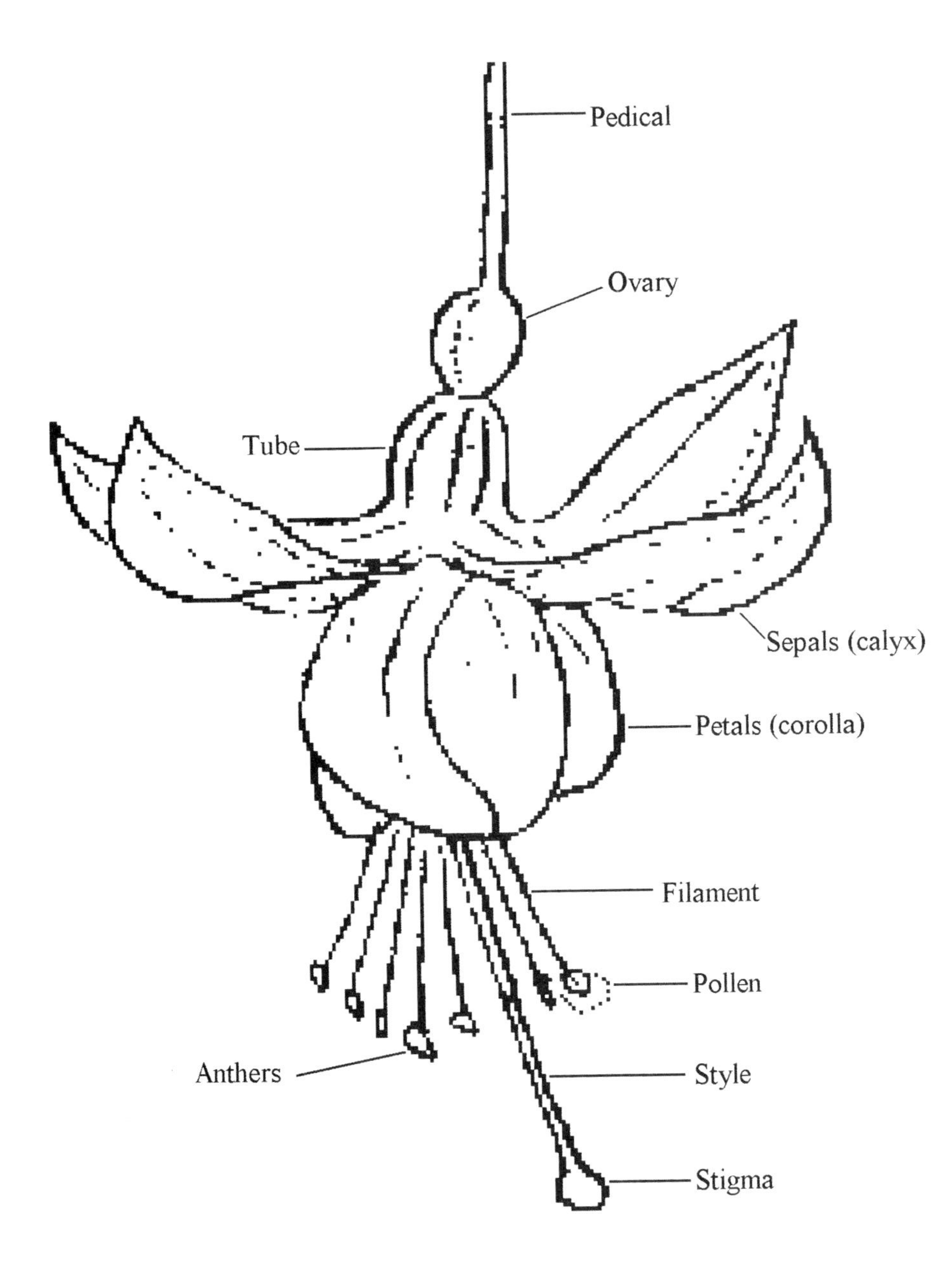
Pedical
Ovary
Tube
Sepals (calyx)
Petals (corolla)
Filament
Pollen
Anthers
Style
Stigma

THE BRITISH FUCHSIA SOCIETY SPECIES SHOW LIST.

This species list is for show purposes only and replaces all previous species show lists. It is not intended to he used as a botanical document; Revisions of this list will take place annually, if necessary. Should any interested reader want to alter the list, contact should be made in writing, with the BFS. Show Committee before September 30th of each year. Notice of any changes will he published in the B.F.S. Spring Bulletin. **Only the species listed below may he shown in the species class at BFS. National Shows.**

F. alpestris.
F. ampliata.
F. andrei.
F. apetala.
F. arborescens.
F. ayavacensis.
F. boliviana.
F. boliviana var. alba.
F. brevilobis.
F. campii.
F. campos-portoi.
F. cinerea.
F. coccinea.
F. crassistipula.
F. cyrtrandroides.
F. decussata.
F. denticulata.
F. dependens.
F. excorticata.
F. fulgens.
F. fulgens var. gesneriana.
F. fulgens var goselli.
F. fulgens var. michoacans.
F. fulgens var. minuata.
F. fulgens var rubra grandiflora.
F. furfuracea.
F. gehrigeri.
F. glazioviana.
F. hartwegii.
F. hatschbachii.
F. inflata.
F. insignis.
F. jimenezii
F. juntasensis.
F. lehmannii.
F. loxensis.
F. lycioides.
F. macrophylla.
F. macrostigma.
F. magdalanae.
F. magellanica.
F. magellanica var. aurea.
F. magellanica var. aurea variegata.
F. magellanica var. comber.
F. magellanica var. conica.
F. magellanica var discolor.
F. magellanica var. globosa.
F. magellanica var. gracilis.
F. magellanica var. longipedunculata.
F. magellanica var macrostema.
F. magellanica var molinae (alba).
F. magellanica var. myrtifolia.
F. magellanica var. pumilla.
F. magellanica var. thompsonii.
F. magellanica var tricolor.
F. magellanica var. versicolor.
F. mathewsii.
F. nigricans.
F. pallescens.

F. paniculata.
F. paniculata ssp mixensis.
F. perscandens.
F. petiolaris.
F. pilaloensis.
F. pringsheimii.
F. procumbens.
F procumbens var. argenteus.
F. procumbens var. variegata.
F. putumayensis.
F. regia.
F. regia ssp regia.
F. regia ssp reitzii.
F. regia ssp serrae.
F. sanctae-rosae.
F. scabriuscula.
F. sessilifolia.
F. simplicicaulis.
F. splendens.
F. splendens / cordifolia.
F. steyermarkii.
F. tilletiana.
F. triphylla.
F. vargasiana.
F. venusta.
F. verrucosa.
F. vulcanica.
F. wurdackii.

THE BRITISH FUCHSIA SOCIETY HARDY LIST

This Hardy list replaces all, previous lists and is for show purposes only.
It does not necessarily mean that the fuchsias listed will survive, when left in the ground, through every winter, in every corner of the United Kingdom. Revisions to this list, if necessary, will take place annually. Should anyone interested wish to suggest alterations to the list, they should do so in writing, to the Show sub-Committee before September 30th each year. Details of any proven hardiness **will** be required with each suggestion, and the B.F.S. Membership as a whole may also be asked for support with regard to a cultivars hardiness in other parts of the country. Notice of any changes will be published in the Society's Spring Bulletin as they occur.
Note: *Any cultivar suggested for the Hardy List* ***must*** *have survived at least* ***five*** *consecutive winters and begun to flower in July or early August.*

Abbe Farges.
Achievement.
Admiration.
Alice Hoffinan.
A.M. Larwick.
Avalanche - *Henderson 1869.*
Baby Blue Eyes.
Bashful.
Beacon.
Beranger.
Blue Bush.
Blue Gown.
Bouquet.
Brilliant.
Brodsworth.
Brutus.
Caledonia.
Cardinal Farges.
Carmen.
C. J. Howlett.
Charming.
Connie.
Chillerton Beauty.
China Lantern.
Cliff's Hardy.
Conspicua.
Constance.
Corallina.
Display.
Doc.
Dollar Princess.
Dopey.
Dorothy.
Drame.
Dr. Foster.
Dunrobin Bedder.
E. A. Babbs.
Edith.
El Cid.
Eleanor Rawlings.
Emile Zola.
Empress of Russia.
Enfant Prodigue.
Falklands.
Flash.
Flashlight.
Florence Turner.
F. magellanica and variants. *alba,. aurea,. gracilis; longipedunculata; prostrata; pumila,. sharpitor,. thompsonii,. tricolor,. variegata*
Garden News.

General Monk.
Genii.
Glow.
Gold Brocade.
Goldsworth Beauty.
Graf Witte.
Grayrigg.
Grumpy.
Happy.
Hawkshead.
Herald.
Herbe de Jacques.
H. A. Brown.
Howlett's Hardy.
Jack Wilson.
Joan Cooper.
Justin's Pride.
Lady Ambersley.
Lady Thumb.
Lena.
Liebriez.
Lilac Dainty.
Mme. Cornelissen.
Margaret.
Margaret Brown.
Margaret Roe.
Margery Blake.
Mauve Wisp.
Mephisto.
Monsieur Thibaut.
Mr. A. Huggett.
Mrs. Popple.
Mrs. W. P. Wood.
Mr. Rundle.
Neue Welt.
Nicola Jane.
Pee Wee Rose.
Papoose.
Phyllis.
Pixie.
Phyrne.
President.
President Elliot.
Prosperity.
Purple Splendour.
Purple Cornelissen.
Reading Show.
Rhombifolia.
Riccartonii.
Robin Hood.
Rose of Castille.
Rose of Castille Improved.
Rufus.
Ruth.
Santa Claus.
Santa Cruz.
Schneewittchen.
Schneewittcher.
Sealand Prince.
Silverdale.
Sleepy.
Sneezy.
Snowcap.
Son of Thumb.
Susan Travis.
Tennessee Waltz.
The Tarns.
Thornley's Hardy.
Timothy Hammett.
Tom Thumb.
Trase.
Tresco.
Trudy.
Voltaire.
White Pixie.
W. P. Wood.
Whiteknights Amethyst.
Whiteknights Blush.
Whiteknights Glister.
Whiteknights Pearl.

Notes

Notes

BRITISH FUCHSIA SOCIETY SALES ITEMS.

The following items are offered for sale. Please contact the Sales Administrator, Mrs Ann Porter, 12 Hazel Grove, Southport. PRS 6AX.

BFS. Lapel Badges

BFS. Car Stickers.

Judges & Exhibitors Handbook

Cultural Leaflets

1. Cultural notes. 2. Hardy. 3. Over-wintering. 4. Pests. 5. Diseases. 6. Standards. 7. Baskets. 8. Triphyllas. 9. Species. 10. Bonsai. 11. Propagation. 12. Encliandra's. 3. Composts.
Discounts for bulk orders, please telephone for details.

BFS. Ties.
Available in the following colours:
Light Green; Beige; Maroon; Green; Brown; Navy; Grey; Blue:

Books Published by the Society.

About The Fuchsia. *An English Translation of the 1844 Edition by Felix Porcher. Translated by Francine Sagar. Edited by J. V Porter.*
This is a translation of the first fuchsia book ever published.

Addendum to the 1991 edition of *The Checklist of Species, Hybrids and Cultivars of the Genus Fuchsia By Leo Boullemier*
This addendum is the authors last published work, and completes his work 1992

Fuchsias of the 19th & Early 20th Century. By Eric A. Johns.
An absolute must for the serious historian or enthusiast.

We also stock some privately published books. A list is available please send SAE.